PRAISE FOR
Team Emotional Intelligence 2.0

"Increasing team emotional intelligence is a must for any group that wants to realize their full potential. This brilliant book provides everything you need to take you and your team to the next level."

—Dr. Travis Bradberry, Chief People Scientist at LEADx and coauthor of *Emotional Intelligence 2.0*

"Dr. Jean Greaves and Evan Watkins show that team emotional intelligence is just as important as strategy and efficiency in making a team great. In this well-researched, highly readable book, you'll learn what it looks like when team EQ is low—and what can be accomplished when team EQ is high. Buy *Team Emotional Intelligence 2.0*, put its action plan to use, and watch your team soar!"

—Ken Blanchard, coauthor of *The New One Minute Manager®* and *High Five! The Magic of Working Together*

"*Team Emotional Intelligence 2.0* is loaded with powerful insights and practical strategies for anyone looking to build stronger emotional intelligence capabilities. The authors have charted a clear path to building awareness, creating connection, and fostering collaboration in ways that help the sum add up to more than the parts. For leaders seeking to learn more about how a group becomes a team—from the neuroscience behind how those relationships come together to regular practices to drive new behaviors—this book is a must read."

—Bryan Power, Chief People Officer, Nextdoor

"There's nothing like learning from an expert—and that's an understatement when it comes to Jean Greaves. *Team Emotional Intelligence 2.0* is packed with examples, strategies, and an action plan that show you how to harness the maximum power of your team's potential."

—Elaine Beich, author of *Skills for Career Success* and *The New Business of Consulting*

"In our highly interdependent world, having high team EQ is essential for getting collaborative work done and achieving great results. Individual EQ served us well in the past, but team EQ is required for performance breakthroughs in the future. Dr. Greaves' insightful book gives us the roadmap on how to do it."

—David Covey, CEO of SMCOVEY, LLC and coauthor of the bestseller *Trap Tales: Outsmarting the 7 Hidden Obstacles to Success*

"*Team Emotional Intelligence 2.0*'s simple, elegant, research-based model and strategies enable leaders to accelerate team connection, unleash innovation, and leverage the gift of people succeeding through deep, meaningful, focused relationships. Set your teams up for success: Give them this framework for insightful conversations that drive excellence and help teams and organizations achieve their desired goals."

—Vicki Halsey, author of *Brilliance by Design*

"As a film and TV producer for over 30 years, I have learned that emotional intelligence is a very important tool for leaders building cohesive and emotionally aware production teams. *Team Emotional Intelligence 2.0* offers invaluable strategies to better understand how to quickly identify EQ issues and fix them. It should be essential reading for all producers, directors, and studio executives as they embark on their productions. It offers invaluable concepts and strategies for those in our field who must take diverse people and content, and then quickly build a cohesive culture and teams for short-term work periods."

—Gary Foster, Film / TV Producer and
co-founder of Humanity on Set

"If you think you've read everything on team development, think again. These authors offer powerful and memorable tips that can help any team and any team leader at any phase."

—Dr. Beverly Kaye, CEO, BevK & Company and
best-selling author of *Love 'Em or Lose 'Em:
How to Get Good People to Stay*

TEAM EMOTIONAL INTELLIGENCE 2.0

THE FOUR ESSENTIAL SKILLS OF HIGH-PERFORMING TEAMS

DR. JEAN GREAVES
EVAN WATKINS

11526 Sorrento Valley Road, Suite A-2

San Diego, CA 92121

For information regarding special discounts for bulk purchases, please contact TalentSmartEQ® at:

888-818-SMART (toll free, US & Canada callers) or 858-509-0582

Visit us online at www.TalentSmartEQ.com

ISBN 978-0-9747193-4-4
First Printing: 2021

OTHER WORKS

Explore these other works about emotional intelligence by Dr. Jean Greaves and the TalentSmartEQ® team:

Emotional Intelligence 2.0®

Co-authored by TalentSmartEQ® founders Dr. Jean Greaves and Dr. Travis Bradberry, this #1 best-selling book has one purpose: increasing your EQ.

The authors provide a step-by-step program for increasing your emotional intelligence via 66 proven strategies that target self-awareness, self-management, social awareness, and relationship management. Includes access to the Emotional Intelligence Appraisal®—Self Assessment to measure your own emotional intelligence and jump-start your EQ journey.

Leadership 2.0®

Co-authored by TalentSmartEQ® founders Dr. Jean Greaves and Dr. Travis Bradberry, this groundbreaking book redefines leadership. *Leadership 2.0* identifies the leadership skills that get results in the workplace.

Includes access to the Leadership 2.0® assessment to measure 22 critical leadership skills, including emotional intelligence.

For everyone who has ever worked on a team.
Your journeys are the inspiration
for this book.

CONTRIBUTORS

Writing this book was also a team effort.
The following subject matter experts made
significant contributions to this book.

Susan DeLazaro, M.S.

Joshua Rosenthal, M.Sc., M.A.

David Brzozowski, B.A.

Howard Farfel, M.B.A.

Sheri Duchock, Ph.D.

Amy Miller, M.S.

CONTENTS

1. Peak Performance   1

2. Team Emotional Intelligence: Why It Matters   15

3. The Four Essential Skills: What Team EQ Looks and Sounds Like   37

4. The Pathway to Team EQ: Your Action Plan   67

5. Emotion Awareness Strategies   75

6. Emotion Management Strategies   105

7. Internal Relationship Strategies   147

8. External Relationship Strategies   183

Epilogue   225

Discussion Questions for Reading Groups and Teams   239

Acknowledgments   243

Notes   245

EQ Resource Guide   265

TEAM EMOTIONAL INTELLIGENCE 2.0

THE FOUR ESSENTIAL SKILLS OF HIGH-PERFORMING TEAMS

1

——

PEAK PERFORMANCE

After months of computer screens and keyboards, Alicia, her younger brother Rob, and their friend Amir could almost smell the pine-fueled mountain air of Yosemite National Park. The three climbers were driving over from San Francisco, their car filled with music, chatter, and jokes. The team of climbers was set to ascend Cathedral Peak the next day, a 10,587-foot mountain named for its granite versions of a sanctuary, turrets, pinnacles, and a spire. Free from final exams at last, they were already charged with spirited emotions—camaraderie, excitement, and anticipation. Alicia, six years older and a seasoned climber, was practically buzzing with confidence and passion, and this rubbed off on Rob and Amir, who were each less experienced than she was.

Getting out of the bay area took hours, so they stopped to

treat themselves to burgers at Rush Creek Lodge. Stopping for dinner broke up the drive and made it so they wouldn't need to cook as they arrived at dusk and pitched their tents. During dinner, Alicia told stories of previous successful climbs in Yosemite.

In step with the plan this team had spent months putting together, they woke up at four in the morning and unzipped their tents only to find that Amir's pack had no food in it. As Amir had rushed to leave his apartment, he'd left the bear canisters he packed sitting on the counter. Being the most inexperienced climber, he had spent quite a bit of time preparing and packing their meals. It was his main contribution to the plan. Of course, the team could go get more food, but this hitch in their plan was inconvenient and subtly changed the tone of their climb from smooth sailing to bumpier waters. A slight sense of pressure and discouragement filled in.

The climbers packed up camp in a hurry and drove to purchase food at the nearest convenience store. Two hours behind schedule, they reached the trailhead where they would begin hiking to the southeast buttress of Cathedral Peak, the starting point of their climb. Their detour to pick up food had pushed back the start of their ascent to 10:00 am instead of 8:00 am. Not ideal, but the team calculated a summit time of 3:00 pm if everything else went smoothly. There was an increased pressure to stick exactly to this adjusted plan and even to try to make up for lost time. The group went silent as they pulled the food out of the trunk and transferred it into their bags. Already, they felt very different than they had on the drive over the evening before. Amir felt terrible for causing this setback. He felt like he had received a guest invite to this climb and wanted to do his best to help it proceed smoothly. Rob felt bad for Amir and was highly sensitized to Alicia, trying to read if she was mad. Alicia, meanwhile, felt frustrated that she trusted a novice to handle something as important as their calories.

Before the team began their hike, they stopped by the ranger station to check the weatherboard. The station was empty, and the day's weather had not been posted. There was no cell service either. Each of them gazed up at the sky, knowing better than to ignore the elements. Weather in the Sierras was notoriously fickle—clear one moment, then cloudy the next. Thankfully, the sky was blue and sunny, no storm in sight.

Crunched for time, Alicia felt like she had to help the group make decisions quickly if they were going to reach the peak. Spurred on by their optimism, they decided that if anything, no information suggested the park staff anticipated no storm. A missing weather report was too minor a problem to be a decisive factor on an otherwise clear day.

Working quickly and silently in an attempt to make up for lost time, the three of them trekked to the base of Cathedral

Peak in a matter of hours.

Alicia chose their climb well. The ascent of Cathedral Peak is considered one of the best beginner-level climbs for its long length, its "grippy" face, the smattering of unique rock knobs,

how easy it is to protect (a climbing tactic to reduce risk), and ultimately the panorama at the summit. Glacier-polished granite mountains in the distance and sequoia trees, lakes, waterfalls, and meadows

John Muir's sketch of Cathedral Peak from his book *My First Summer in the Sierra.*

at closer range made for a sight so breathtaking that it floored even the seasoned mountaineer John Muir back in 1869. He described the view, writing, "It was the first time I've ever been to church in California."

The first pitch (rope length) of their climb could not have gone smoother. The trio made their way up in good time and began the second. Settling into a groove with one another, they climbed slowly but surely, with only a few words of technical advice from Alicia as they went.

Though Rob and Amir had known each other for three years already, and Amir had spent holidays with Rob, Alicia, and their family, this group of friends was brand new as a climbing

4

team. Each person felt quite different as the trip approached. For Rob and Amir, both relatively inexperienced, the climb would be a challenge and ultimately a personal record—neither of them had ever climbed more than one pitch, and this was five. Also, Amir was flying home the following night, so this was their one shot. As the experienced rock climber and someone who had successfully climbed for ten years, Alicia came to this climb with confidence and an existing mental and physical model of how to approach a route of this difficulty. She knew what types of ropes, anchors, nuts, cams, carabiners, and quickdraws to use across a variety of situations. It was Alicia who influenced their plan the most, as Rob and Amir deferred to her and her experience.

It wasn't until the team finished the second pitch that a thin layer of clouds filled in over the valley, thickening and darkening with time. Eight hours into a day that had already delivered two more hiccups than anticipated, stress began to cloud their minds and make their hearts beat faster, though this was easily mistaken for the physical efforts they were putting in. Amir and Rob both wondered to themselves what Alicia thought of the shade of clouds. A storm was approaching.

Friction finally bubbled up between Alicia and Rob when Amir asked what direction the clouds might head. Alicia, feeling responsible for Amir's once-in-a-lifetime opportunity, announced that, based on the clouds' advancing rate, they could forge ahead and finish before any rain started. Rob patted more chalk on his sweaty hands and felt his back clench up the way it always did when his nerves peaked. Personally, he leaned toward throwing in the towel and mentioned to Alicia that, in his opinion, the climb was already a success, and the views from the third pitch were already incredible. Alicia reassured him, in a well-traveled older sister way, that she felt sure they could make it before the rain arrived. Rob wasn't about to use this moment to pick a fight with her experience and status. She was more knowledgeable and had looked after his safety many times over the years. Rob accepted her reassurance and joined forces with her to reassure Amir.

During final exams, Amir had privately gone online to read reviews of the climb and knew the mountain's potential for lightning. A quick search of Cathedral Peak online informed him that, "It's a great big lightning rod—get off ASAP if thunder comes your way." Recalling this, he was preoccupied with fear now, his hands trembling with adrenaline. He wanted nothing more than to descend. Yet, he also felt too embarrassed to admit this, especially after messing up his one simple responsibility. Amir agreed out loud that the views from here were hard to beat, hoping his already fulfilled climbing needs might convince Rob and Alicia it was okay to descend. However, as the least experienced member of the group, he didn't feel comfortable enough to ask or demand them to stop on his behalf. *For all I know, he told himself, this kind of thing just happens on climbs, and Alicia understands the distance and timing better than my nerves do.*

After a bit of back-and-forth between the three about whether to continue or descend, they agreed as a team to keep pushing. As the sky grew darker and rain became visible in the valley, their stress and self-induced pressure to finish propelled them forward. Without further discussion, the trio silently pressed on, feeling focused, excited, and scared as they raced to beat the rain to the summit. Zooming in on each of the climbers, you would see that they all wore similarly determined and anxious expressions. As they communicated, their body language and facial expressions were in sync. They hardly needed to speak.

Each foot of altitude sapped a bit more oxygen from their brains, and their adrenaline surged as they gazed down the side of the cliff with nothing but ropes and metal to support them. The team made it to the fifth and final pitch just as the clouds caught up. The rock face slickened immediately. Then came the rain, then hail. They could barely see, their control of their hands diminished in the cold, and the ice pelting against the granite made it tough to hear one another. Finally, Alicia, as the lead, reached the summit, and Rob and Amir had just the last stretch.

That's when Rob and Amir felt all their hair stand on end.

> **A thunderhead had locked onto their bodies, and there was nothing they could do. Everything around them started to buzz and hum like a swarm of wasps.**

A thunderhead had locked onto their bodies, and there was nothing they could do. Everything around them started to buzz and hum like a swarm of wasps.

Spurred by an instinct to flee, Rob and Amir scrambled up the wet face toward an overhanging rock, a flat spot in case they were struck. As feared, lightning struck, with multiple prongs, and slammed Rob into the wall in front of him. He heard Amir moan to his left and saw Alicia unconscious up at the storm-shrouded summit. Rob clambered recklessly up the rest of the face to the summit to help his sister. It was just past 3:00 pm, and, planning to descend that afternoon, they had no tools to start a fire, no way to treat Alicia's burns, and no waterproof clothing to avoid hypothermia through the night.

Luckily, another climber at the base who was planning to climb the next day heard them yelling to each other and used her ham radio to call for help. Alicia, Rob, and Amir were rescued that evening and all survived. Each of them admitted later on that they weren't sure why they had endangered their lives in pursuit of their goal.

When Emotions Run Your Team, and Your Team Runs into Trouble

The Cathedral Peak team, though tight-knit and led by an experienced climber, didn't know how to interpret one of the most important, frequent, and powerful pieces of data available to them: their emotions. They found a nice balance and rhythm with their physical skills as they summited, but they failed to find the same balance and rhythm with another equally important skill set during their climb—their team emotional intelligence (team EQ).

The emotions and rational thoughts among a team can work in concert, or they can work in stark opposition. For this team, as with many teams, their emotions dominated their every move, powering their decisions and actions and propelling them up the peak. That's the confusing nature of emotions. At times, this team's feelings worked in their favor, and at other times, their feelings worked against them. The rush of elevated emotions helped drive the team to accomplish a five-pitch climb, something two team members had never done before. Those same elevated emotions also drove their unrealistically optimistic analysis of the missing weather report and caused them to mislabel their last push as a race against something as benign as rain.

This team's emotions were not always in harmony. At

times, their emotions were out of sync, which also affected their performance negatively. Though all three climbers noticed warning signs building in their environment, and noticed feelings building internally, they didn't pause long enough to listen to what their own emotions were telling them or to hear each other out. Rob and Amir under communicated their hesitancies and offloaded all the responsibility on Alicia. Meanwhile, Alicia spent no time reviewing her own feelings or absorbing theirs. She believed that her previous wins as a climber and her role as "caring older sister" would prevail. Her past climbing successes were so smooth that she had never had to turn back. The thought of doing so was unfamiliar. In their last moment of crisis, as lightning struck, Rob and Amir each let their fear get the best of their good judgment and scrambled recklessly up the exposed rock face.

While your team may not be climbing storm-prone mountains, there's a good chance that, like the Cathedral Peak team, your team allows individual and group emotions to take the driver's seat more often than you want and realize. Your team members experience feelings throughout your workday, and those feelings are clamoring to get everyone's attention as you talk together, problem solve, think abstractly, and devise plans. Unnoticed, misunderstood, or unmanaged, a team's emotions can lead to hasty actions at the expense of sound, rational thought. Often, we later regret these actions, like moving ahead without a weather report, dashing up a rock face in a thunderstorm, or making an impulsive decision that consumes over a year of your team's work only to yield mediocre results.

Alicia, Rob, and Amir ignored, suppressed, or dealt privately with important emotions (like skepticism, pressure, worry, and fear) that surfaced throughout the day. These feelings signaled them to take notice of and discuss approaching danger. Each of them noticed these feelings bubbling up but ultimately did not attend to them effectively enough to glean anything meaningful. This was partially because they were focused on other feelings—excitement, desire to impress, hesitancy to push back, and insecurity—and partially because they didn't recognize how important their emotions were as resources for the team's performance. Emotions were felt but not heeded. They disregarded the feelings and relationship dynamics that could protect them and paid too much attention to the feelings and relationship dynamics that led them straight into danger.

To be fair, emotions are not always easy to read. At an individual level, it takes practice to become aware of moments when you should attend more to your feelings than your thoughts and become skilled at doing so. When you add this to the complexity of an entire team trying to navigate a life-and-death situation while emotions spread from person to person and relationships interfere with logic, the challenges of making sense of emotions multiply. Teams have a lot more data to read and a lot more emotions, actions, and interactions to manage. Your team's ability to effectively read these emotions, feelings, and moods is the foundation of team emotional intelligence.

Every Team's Journey

Team Emotional Intelligence 2.0 has one purpose—developing your group's team EQ skills to maximize your team performance. This book will get you started on what you and your teammates need to know about this crucial skill set and how to begin putting these skills into practice.

It's time the veil is pulled back on the mystery of high-performing teams that somehow build strong bonds, get unstuck, rise to challenges, and achieve their goals without falling prey to negative team dynamics. This book covers key research findings on the influence that emotions have on team effectiveness and performance outcomes. These pages introduce the four essential team EQ skills that help teams excel and illustrate what weak and strong team EQ look and sound like on teams across industries.

Most importantly, actionable team EQ strategies reveal specifics for what you and your team can do to increase your team emotional intelligence. We incorporated the research and our experience working with teams into recommended actions that any team can practice together. The strategies are designed to help you notice, understand, and manage your group's emotions and build strong bonds both within and outside your team.

If there's one thing to internalize before you work through this book, it's this: Team emotional intelligence can be developed with deliberate practice. Using the information and guidance in the following chapters, select and practice the team EQ strategies that will best equip your team to excel.

Your team's emotions and relationships can work in your team's favor, or they can hold you back. We invite you to leverage team EQ know-how to maximize your group's collective knowledge, strengths, and potential.

2

—

TEAM EMOTIONAL INTELLIGENCE: WHY IT MATTERS

There is no question that people working in teams in this century will have to navigate disruption and change, and rapidly. Technology adoption, digital transformation, globalization, virtual and hybrid teamwork, and updating social contracts to support the well-being of people at work were all named as top priorities for workforce planning by chief human resource officers. Ten of 15 industry sectors and 24 of 25 countries ranked emotional intelligence (EQ) in their top 15 high-demand skill sets for the future, and those that didn't named resilience, flexibility, and stress tolerance—each more achievable with increased self-awareness and emotion control, two core emotional intelligence skills. The people at work who are able to notice how they feel and then act on these feelings in ways that are constructive for them, their coworkers, and their organizations will be in high demand.

Despite the recognized and ongoing value of individual emotional intelligence skills to organizations worldwide, important insights emerging about team emotional intelligence are not yet widely familiar to people who are members of a team. As social beings, we listen, learn, pass around information, and produce more effectively in smaller interconnected groups. Imagine a company of 10,000 people with no teams at all! It would be chaos. Group chat rooms and virtual meetings would freeze under the load. Imagine how you would get your work done without the team you are currently on or the teams that work alongside yours. You would feel lonely, disconnected, maybe even a little lost. That's why it is critical for teams to not only exist but also for team members to understand how to interact and work well together.

At TalentSmartEQ, we have devoted decades to training and testing EQ, reaching over 2 million people on their individual EQ skills and thousands of team members on their team EQ skills. Our trainers have observed countless intact teams gather to interact and talk about how emotions impact their teams' work. We learned first-hand that people on teams are hungry for help with how to handle their groups' emotions and relationships. We hear team members grapple with what to do when intense feelings escalate, and everyone's watching. We listen to their wish for guidance when the feelings of a few overpower the rest, and resentment builds toward unspoken rules that dictate what team members can and can't say about how they feel at work. Moods can be palpable during team meetings, but few team members are comfortable talking about them. Even weariness is mentioned as a challenge by many teammates who listen to other teammates criticize yet a third teammate without any plan to resolve the issue.

These observations and challenges all point to the need for a discussion of emotions, feelings, and moods in team settings. Every team can leverage useful insights on how to understand what emotions are, how they operate in group settings, and what the research shows so far about how emotional intelligence at the team level improves team performance.

Emotions, Feelings, and Moods

People working in teams use data to do all kinds of productive work. They use information to produce, advise, problem solve, deliver, discover, serve, entertain, care for, govern, teach, build, compete, and create—just to name a few types of work that would suffer without access to their relevant data. The quantity and quality of supporting information available to a team have important implications for success or failure.

Emotions, feelings, and moods are high-quantity and high-quality mind and body data available to every team. Yet, this nuanced information is waiting to be welcomed to many a team's table for attention, analysis, and use in their teamwork. Whether ignored or not properly understood, a team's emotions can be the difference between injury by lightning or summiting Cathedral Peak on a different, better day. Team emotional intelligence can also make all the difference in your team as you attempt to achieve your important goals and as emotional data streams in.

> **Emotions, feelings, and moods are high-quantity and high-quality mind and body data available to every team.**

Emotions, feelings, and moods each offer valuable information. Emotions are the neural activity generated in your brain's limbic system (located at the center of the brain) in response to opportunities and threats around you. Emotions send signals to your brain and body's neuromuscular, cardiovascular, hormonal, and cognitive systems to influence your thoughts and behaviors. Based on the environment you work in and the people you work with, your emotions physically tell your mind and body whether conditions are ripe for you to concentrate, push harder, be present, argue, worry, be on alert, collaborate, take risks, engage, rest, or celebrate. These are just some of the many activities you need to know when and how to participate in as a team member. Emotions are physical data intended to help you and your teammates survive and excel at work.

Feelings and moods are descriptions we use to give meaning to our emotional experiences. People perceive a variety of emotions similarly and give these feelings labels such as disappointed, pleased, preoccupied, or proud. So, for example, when a team member says they feel disappointed, others on the team will be able to draw on their own experiences of disappointment to empathize. Moods refer to feeling states that are typically less intense and less specific than emotions and feelings, and they persist for longer periods (anywhere from about an hour to days). Think of moods as a blend of emotions and feelings that follow you around for a while to remind you and others, if anyone were to look closely, that there may be something you or your team should attend to.

Emotions, feelings, and moods are each valuable mental and physical data trying to grab your team's attention so you can optimize your next steps. If only Rob had read his nerves and sweaty hands as unusual for him. Then, he could have shared with Amir that these signs might indicate that they should descend early. This, in turn, would have given Amir permission to share what he read online, and he could have stepped in to offer his whole-hearted agreement that they should turn back. Two united team members able to assess and share their emotions may have broken through to Alicia.

One person experiences a range of emotions and interactions every day, so when it comes to your team, the number of emotions and interactions to collectively grapple with multiplies. A team that is high in team emotional intelligence is often described with intangibles such as "great team culture," "special," or "the kind of team that somehow rises above the sum of its parts." That is because high team EQ groups are more in tune with their emotions, feelings, and moods. As a result, they are better set to respond productively as a cohesive unit. Doing so hour-to-hour, day-to-day, and month-to-month has a cumulative effect on their work and how they work together.

> **One person experiences a range of emotions and interactions every day, so when it comes to your team, the number of emotions and interactions to collectively grapple with multiplies.**

Our Social Brain: How It Works

Although collaborating successfully through a deluge of emotional data sounds complicated, it's actually the very thing that we're wired to do. The human brain is wired for social connection with specialty neurons called mirror and spindle neurons.

Mirror neurons are a class of neurons that help our mind respond to the actions we observe other people doing, helping to determine their intentions and next actions. Mirror neurons help team members interact and work together to develop a "we-radar" and a "we-mindset" by sensing subtle and sophisticated interac-

> **Mirror neurons help team members interact and work together over time to develop a "we-radar" and a "we-mindset."**

tions as we watch, listen, feel, and interact with each other. For example, mirror neurons allow us to watch someone dance and then imitate them, and they allow us to see someone feeling and feel it for ourselves. Mirror neurons help ensure teams are not just individuals working side by side but a group tuned into each other as they work together.

The special spindle neuron is larger, elongated (four times longer than other brain cells and neurons!), and tapered at both ends, like a spindle. These cells also reside in the limbic system and become active when we express our emotions, give our attention, and regulate our moods.

Spindle neurons help our brain monitor and react to the gut feeling sensations our body sends when we feel social emotions such as empathy, guilt, trust, love, embarrassment, and humor. Their sizable length allows them to operate as a high-speed communication line, able to send messages to other parts of the brain faster. This was likely a survival advantage that helped us make fast, intuitive decisions about emotionally charged situations: who to trust and what to do next.

Our primitive brains interpret our social connections as matters of survival. So much so that the pain center in our brain is activated when others hurt our feelings. Hurt feelings alert our minds to an important social connection that may be weakening or broken. They instruct us to attend to whether we may be less valuable to a person or group than we thought or would like. We then focus on what to say or do to reestablish the strength of that connection. This explains why hearing about a meeting you weren't invited to can unravel your confidence in your status as a valued team member, even when the reason was a busy coworker who typed too fast and hit send without realizing you were not on the list.

This same primitive social brain also compels us to get to know other people and take steps to strengthen the bonds we feel with one another so we can access each other to meet the challenges that will come our way. Consider the amazing ways people master social interactions and put them to good use:

1. **We can read others:** From the moment we are born, we rely on constant attention from adults to survive. In those early years, we are constantly learning about emotions and social cues—facial expressions, verbal cues, language, and body language.

2. **We can build community:** Social skills built our societies and our cultures. It was our ancestors' social skills that enabled them to successfully hunt big game in groups (using hand signals, whispers, and words) and to record and pass on their knowledge of agriculture through generations (with stories and writing). Eventually, they produced much more food than they needed to survive. Surplus food meant free time to develop the makings of culture—traditions, sciences, and arts, which we participate in as we join and build communities.

3. **We can learn better together:** Social skills help us achieve more academically. Research comparing students working together (called cooperative learning) with students working individually show increased motivation and persistence, more positive attitudes, work completed faster,

better memory of what they learned, and higher average achievement. Prior grades and performances were no longer predictive of how well students would perform when learning cooperatively and socially.

4. **We can accomplish more together:** Social skills drive human innovation and knowledge. For example, Neil Armstrong has the distinction of being the first person on the moon, but he couldn't do it alone. Landing on the moon required an incredible number of people on multiple teams with a wide range of expertise. Rocket scientists specialized in the construction of the launch pad, while computer engineers, software engineers, technicians, and geologists identified a landing spot on the moon. Specialized tailors developed their life-support suits. The list is a long one. No single person could master all these skills and knowledge in their lifetime, but through collaboration, teams of highly specialized experts were able to send Neil and his crew to the moon.

Team Emotional Intelligence

Social skills are a kind of superpower capable of lifting the collective performance of a team beyond the sum of each team member's capability. Social skills operate more like a multiplier, a way to far exceed the abilities of individual superstars at your organization.

The paradox about our social brain and teamwork is this: Social skills come to us naturally, yet we frequently undervalue their power and complexity and overvalue the individual. Think about the sports team that cracks under pressure in the playoffs, the sales team that competes with one another instead of sharing tips and collaborating, or the team struggling to adapt to the changes or workloads on their horizon. These challenges are less about talent and knowledge than they are about how team members feel and how they work to manage their emotions and relationships. In other words, it is a matter of team emotional intelligence.

Team emotional intelligence places the group's emotions and social interactions top of mind and squarely in the hands of the whole team. The team manages how they feel and how they connect as they work together to excel. Their efforts help them to become more aware of their emotional habits and tendencies, to respond constructively

> **Team emotional intelligence places the group's emotions and social interactions top of mind and squarely in the hands of the whole team. The group manages how they feel and how they connect as they work together to excel.**

when these tendencies get in their way, and to build healthy relationships inside and outside the team's boundaries. Of course, team members do not need to feel the same way about situations or people, but their emotions can work well together if they are clear on what they feel (awareness) and how they communicate and act on this effectively (management).

These efforts require skills, which can be developed. Four essential team EQ skills help your team make the most of your natural social wiring and unlock your unique collaborative potential. The first two skills, emotion awareness and emotion management skills, will increase your team's ability to read and act on the emotional, sensory data available to you. The second two skills, internal relationship skills and external relationship skills, will strengthen the bonds your team has with each other and with other people and teams in the arena where your team plays. Team emotional intelligence skills embody a group's ability to manage emotions under stress, build trust, and come together as a cohesive unit when it matters most. They also represent the necessary connections your team must make inside and outside the group to access resources and support and to influence people and decisions that affect your work. Groups with strong team EQ skills work diligently to understand one another, attend to the negative tendencies that hinder progress, and rely on team members' strengths to better face challenges and to foster a supportive team environment.

Better Team EQ, Better Team Performance

The link between feelings, teamwork, and performance can be described as follows: Emotions surface during group interactions to influence team dynamics and relationships, which, in turn, influence the team's effectiveness and ability to achieve team goals. Team EQ skills offer team members proactive words to say and actions to take to help stabilize and manage their dynamics. The following evidence suggests that when team members make the effort to notice emotions at the group

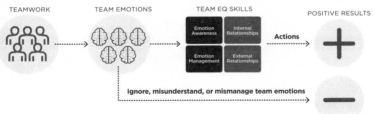

level and proactively do something about them, they perform better than they would if they simply asked each team member to work on their people skills.

An important repeatable finding is that moods transfer among team members and impact team effectiveness. In studies using a trained actor to enact a feeling around other members in a group, the enacted emotion was soon found among group members. This was found when measured by outside observers and when group members reported their own moods. Interestingly, positive emotions spread among group members were found to improve cooperation, decrease conflict, and increase task performance. There are also instances where positive emotions can spread among a group to create feelings of overconfidence and invulnerability. Pressure to feel the same way can then lead to overpromising and underdelivering. Team EQ is about raising awareness among team members that both positive and negative feelings can spread, and it's about helping

the group spot when and how to encourage or manage those emotions in service of reaching their goals.

Recent workplace studies illustrate how team EQ offers gains in outcomes important to specific industries. At a government agency, team EQ increased trust, goal achievement, cross-functional collaboration, and speed. In a study of software development teams facing high-stress projects with extreme deadlines, researchers found that team EQ skills effectively built trust between team members and decreased their overall stress levels. Nurses have notoriously rough schedules and high rates of stress and burnout. In a study conducted on 23 nursing teams, the teams skilled at managing group emotions had greater group cohesion and patient-care outcomes. Patients rated the teams who were better able to manage emotions higher in overall care.

Across industries, teams are recognizing the value of diversity to a team's performance and also seeking ways to navigate differences of opinion and perspective. Team research offers some insights. For 88 cross-functional sourcing teams especially diverse in personalities and attitudes, researchers found they were more likely to experience misaligned goals and problems with overcoming obstacles. Team member differences created conflicts that got in the way of their work. Those teams with higher team EQ scores worked more effectively through their differences to see each other's perspectives.

Another study looked at a process for harnessing diversity to achieve creative outcomes. Interdisciplinary science teams working on climate change were arranged to be diverse in thought and team member backgrounds. Through a designed six-month process, team discussions alternated between emphasizing both where their ideas differed and where they converged. After assessments, interviews, and analysis of comments made by team members, researchers concluded that diversity, though a potential source of conflict in the team, was turned into an asset through congenial collaboration among teammates. The scientists felt their creative outcomes relied on team members feeling respected and able to move back and forth between agreeing and disagreeing with each other's very different ideas.

Emotionally intelligent teams create team trust, and that trust builds collaboration and higher levels of creativity. One study tracked 78 teams of 4–7 members developing marketing plans or real-world marketing research projects. Analyses showed that management of one's emotions and management of others' emotions influenced team trust scores (being relied on for competence and ability) and collaborative culture scores. The trust and collaboration scores predicted project creativity scores. When team members managed their own emotions and those of their team members to examine all sides of an argument during decision-making, they were rated as trusted and their projects more creative.

Team emotional intelligence behaviors offer a wide variety of actions teams can take as they navigate whether their work requires them to collaborate, debate, decide, or create. Team EQ can help your team overcome personality clashes, disparate attitudes, and different ways of dealing with emotions to perform well together.

Team Leaders: Help Is Around You

One of the reasons this book was written for team members rather than team leaders is team leaders can't do it alone. Teams can make a wise investment in the diversity of resources available within their group (skills, temperaments, talents, preferences). Team leaders do not have total responsibility for the emotional climate within the team, though they do have an important share. Team leaders can participate as a team member when applying any of the team EQ strategies in chapters 5–8. They can introduce team EQ to their team to give everyone a common language for understanding and managing team emotions and relationships. Team leaders can also accept support from team members when they initiate and engage with these strategies.

The uniquely important part of the team leader's role is their responsibility to set the emotional tone for the team.

> **The uniquely important part of the team leader's role is their responsibility to set the emotional tone for the team.**

Just as moods transfer among people within a group, team members absorb the team leader's emotions. A repeatable finding in the research shows that followers absorb and remember negative emotional displays from their leaders. Team members spend energy tuning in and reading the team leader's mood, as it holds information for the team about when to relax and feel energized and when the team may need to be concerned or alert.

What this means for every team leader is this: your team's performance will benefit when you also work on your individual EQ skills. When you become more self-aware, you'll discover which of your moods affect your team positively and negatively. When you learn to self-manage, you can reassure your team that your bad mood shouldn't worry or distract them. When you work on your social awareness skills, this will help you know when and how to speak up at a team meeting. For example, you'll know to say things like, "If you saw me looking frustrated after Q2 numbers were reported this morning, it's only because our team's results didn't make it in there. There's still time, and I'm looking forward to this team getting the visibility we deserve." Team members who were worried something much worse had just happened may let out a big sigh of relief as they relax and return to work.

There is one additional responsibility the team leader holds above and beyond those of team members. For those situations where difficulties among team members are not resolved, or one team member's performance suffers for reasons beyond emotions and relationships, team leaders may have to step in. Performance management (defining role responsibilities, communicating priorities, and supervising output) is the team leader's tool for guiding the actual work and correcting repeated problems. That is not a team effort. Similarly, for struggles between team members that are not resolving on their own or with team efforts, the team leader may offer to join a discussion or seek advice for next steps from human resources or legal advisors.

Cross-functional Teams Have Dual Roles

Cross-functional, cross-department, and multi-discipline teams are made up of team members that have more than one affiliation. Each person is a member of the cross-functional team and also a member or team leader of another team. Executive teams, the leadership team, and management teams also have roles on more than one team. Can they really be considered a team? They meet and interact regularly, they do work together, and make decisions together. They definitely have bonded relationships and work toward common goals.

For team emotional intelligence purposes, all types of cross-functional and leadership teams are considered intact teams. Here's why. Members of leadership and cross-functional teams operate in very different worlds, typically departments. They are the team leader of at least one team in that world, and perhaps lead layers of teams. So, dual-role teams represent the closest intersection and ongoing contact between diverse and interconnected teams across the organization. The internal relationships with other leaders are simultaneously their internal and external relationships. This makes these teams a unique case for team emotional intelligence skills, and these teams exist because that interconnection contains such a powerfully positive potential for organizational growth.

What makes a cross-functional team's approach to selecting and practicing team EQ skills and strategies different from other teams is the added responsibility to determine which strategies to emphasize and for what reasons. There may be a false urge to think the whole point to team EQ is to achieve harmony. That's not necessarily the case. Team EQ skills and strategies are intended for healthy relationships to ensure performance excellence and the achievement of goals. Team

EQ skills help members of cross-functional and leadership teams optimize which emotions to attend to or tolerate and how in pursuit of the organization's goals.

Cross-functional and leadership teams must navigate especially tough decisions, difficult conversations, conflicts, unknowns, and changes on the horizon. Though strategies such as having a healthy respect for differences or hearing each other out are important, leadership team members also have to learn when their voice is better heard supporting another team member's voice. Just because one team member has the ability to win people over and wants the team they represent to have influence, it doesn't mean their voice should be the one that wins. It may be another department's know-how that should be supported. When one dual-role team member's idea gets passed over, it's not personal. It's departmental, professional, or cross-functional business. Leaders on executive teams must participate in decisions that feed resources to other teams and then communicate these decisions to their own team.

There is inherent conflict in figuring out what's best for the organization and what's best for each functional team. Cross-functional and leadership team members have to move in and out of different seats, their sense of "we" changing with the perspective each seat requires. Emotions and relationships are complex already. Adding dual team member roles requires courage and close attention to whether you are

Cross-functional and leadership team members have to move in and out of different seats, their sense of "we" changing with the perspective each seat requires.

seeking agreement or support from each other. These can be very different. Leadership and cross-functional teams must be mindful of the challenges on their shoulders. They must find and embrace the team EQ strategies that will drive outcomes and achieve goals, all while attending to the health of the combined internal-external relationships on which they rely.

Whether you are a member of one team, a team leader, or a member of a special type of dual-role team, fully explore the four essential team EQ skills in this book, as they will exercise your social brain as you contribute to the work of your team. Place them as valuable tools in your teamwork tool kit and put them to good use as often as you can.

3

—

THE FOUR ESSENTIAL SKILLS: WHAT TEAM EQ LOOKS AND SOUNDS LIKE

To improve your team's emotional intelligence skills, you first need to understand each of the four skills and what they look like in action. The four core team EQ skills are similar to emotional intelligence skills, but there is one important difference: Team EQ skills are about what team members do on behalf of their group.

It is helpful to break them into two primary competency areas: emotions and relationships. Team emotion competence is made up of your team's emotion awareness and management skills. Together, they enable your team to navigate your group's emotional rhythms as you interact across a wide range of situations and contexts, in person and remotely. Relationship competence is made up of the quality of your team's relationships with each other and with people outside the team.

Awareness of your team's emotions and emotional tendencies (emotion awareness) helps your group to recognize their impact in the moment and to effectively respond when feelings surface and influence team dynamics or the work (emotion management). By building and fostering positive working relationships within the team over time (internal relationships), team members are better equipped to build relationships and influence others outside the team (external relationships).

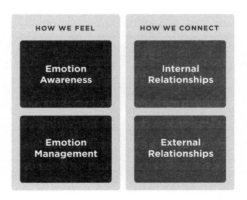

The four essential skills that together make up team emotional intelligence. The first two skills, emotion awareness and emotion management, are about how a team recognizes, understands, and manages its emotions. The second two skills, internal relationships and external relationships, are more about how team members connect with each other and other people outside the team, including other teams.

The following pages offer a window into what each of the four team emotional intelligence skills look and sound like in action. We reviewed thousands of comments from hundreds of teams who completed a team EQ assessment, looking for patterns and trends. For each skill, we have put together representative teams and their comments to illustrate team emotional intelligence when present or skilled and when absent or unhealthy. These team EQ profiles illustrate the variety of ways team emotional intelligence can be exercised or ignored. No single comment represents the full experience of working on a team. However, together they bring high and low team EQ skills to life through specific examples of words, actions, and feelings.

Emotion Awareness

Becoming more aware of team emotions enables your group to accurately understand team members' feelings as they happen. Emotion awareness also enables your team to recognize your tendencies for responding to people and situations. When you invest time in exploring your group's emotional habits and tendencies, you will better grasp how your feelings influence your work together. Then you can decide more accurately how to manage these dynamics.

Emotion awareness is not about digging up uncomfortable feelings or asking people to share personal information they consider private. It is about your group developing an appreciation and understanding of how you react across a variety of circumstances. What, for example, makes your team feel motivated or stuck, confident or stressed, hopeful or discouraged? Teams high in emotion awareness know what they do well and what inspires their best performance. They are also alert to which moods carry them away or take them off track and how.

Emotion awareness is the building block for operating with a high team EQ. When your team learns to become more aware of the feelings within the team, the other team emotional intelligence skills are much easier to work on. If your emotion awareness increases, team member satisfaction also increases. This is made evident by reported feelings of respect, belonging, and productivity on team surveys. Why is this so? When your team feels comfortable expressing how you feel and observing how your teammates feel, you won't just see emotions as uncontrollable or distracting. Instead, your team

When your team learns to become more aware of the feelings within the team, the other team emotional intelligence skills are much easier to work on.

will develop a nuanced radar for emotions, recognizing and understanding them as important signals or data to cue into rather than forces to avoid or ignore. A team with high emotion awareness is far more likely to find calm under stress, put team member strengths to work, and—perhaps most importantly—keep negative emotions from holding the group back.

What Emotion Awareness Sounds Like

Government Sector Team
Emotion awareness score = 91*

What team members say:

"First of all, the fact that there is this team is a success—very diverse, very different from all over the state of Wisconsin. Erik is the commensurate thinker. Melissa is intuitive and smart. Julianne keeps us organized. Nathan senses when we need a pizza run but also powers through."

"Most of the team voices their emotions and frustrations during initial discussions, but they also listen. After they have talked through their frustrations, they leave the emotions out and together agree on a solution."

"We enjoy being with each other, are a very close-knit group, and are sensitive to each other's feelings. If someone has an issue going on, we all try to help, even if not asked. When a member of the team suffers, we all suffer."

"Emotions themselves are not a negative, so I'm glad we haven't let them adversely affect our performance. All emotions are genuinely identified, understood, and considered."

*Scores are on a 100-point scale from the Emotional Intelligence Appraisal®—Team Edition. Scores and comments are from actual teams, though names and identifying information have been altered.

Clinical Care Team
Emotion awareness score = 95

What team members say:

"Before the start of the shift, we each share what is going on in our lives. It helps us be more aware of each other when adverse patient situations occur. The peer support here is one of the best I've experienced. By being able to admit that we don't know everything, we are willing to listen and learn."

"During some shifts, things get extremely hectic, and chaos can enter the picture. Our team always seems to pitch in though."

"Sometimes patient-care team members will get emotional while telling a story or listening to someone else's story, and I think we do a good job letting people express feelings freely and within a safe environment."

"Each team member feels comfortable sharing positive and negative feelings and feedback in a reasonable way. I have to give credit to our Clinical Director, who creates regular opportunities for us to freely communicate at meetings."

"As a team, we do well when one of us is down. We try to lift that person up. We're very tuned in to the emotions of our fellow teammates and take the time to listen and help the other person resolve their dilemma."

What a Lack of Emotion Awareness Sounds Like

Digital Services Team
Emotion awareness score = 59

What team members say:

"Our serious underlying problems are never discussed. I wish we could have more candid conversations. We avoid difficult issues to avoid emotional outcomes. Let's just admit that we avoid anyone who upsets us rather than sharing how we feel about what they're saying or doing."

"I don't know what caused our general mistrust, but usually, it's about feelings. When there are strong feelings in the room, no one acknowledges them. Shouldn't we feel okay to discuss things directly with everyone involved?"

"I wish the team could notice the atmosphere when it is interfering. Then we would know what we are grappling with and address it. However, I realize this kind of process takes extra time."

"I hope the group planning the team activities knows that some of us do not like and feel bad standing up and talking to everyone on the spot. Some of us are good with it, but many of us are not. Just recognize and acknowledge other people's emotions. We need to stop assuming what others feel."

Academic Affairs Team
Emotion awareness score = 67

What team members say:

"Most team members feel left in the dark, confused, and misunderstood. I wish there was a safe space to discuss these feelings."

"I think we make decisions too early just to avoid conflict. People are reluctant to share a thought or constructive criticism because of another's potential reaction. Someone's mood can change the tone of the day. We need to hear all opinions rather than just the most forcefully expressed ones."

"I wish our group could handle the stress better. We put our game faces on and ignore relationships to produce when pressure runs high."

"We don't feel comfortable enough to share our real thoughts. When we do, we often end up feeling attacked or pointed out. I don't like that some people feel they can't share in front of others."

"We tend to focus on getting the job done rather than seeing how everyone is doing."

"Questions during discussions tend to result in defensive reactions rather than appreciation for diversity of thinking to determine the best resolution. I wish the team could be more open and give each other a chance to express our views and respect each other's knowledge."

Emotion Management

Emotion management refers to how your team members behave in response to the moods and emotions that surface within your group. The emotion management skill set includes your team's ability to respond to emotionally uncomfortable situations and influence emotions in constructive ways. This means getting ahead of moments when emotions build with the potential to take over your group, as well as intervening when they do.

This skill set is more nuanced than each team member handling their own emotions. It's possible for your team members to have moderate to healthy EQ skills and for your group to still miss out on the benefits that team EQ has to offer. Think of the team where each person is solely focused on their own behavior and relationships. Those people may act for the most part with emotional intelligence but still sit passively and do relatively little to step in

Thinking and acting on what benefits the team dynamic requires the "we-radar" and "we-mindset," watching for and thinking about what each team member can do or not do to help your group and your group's performance.

and help their team manage group emotions and dynamics. Thinking and acting on what benefits the team dynamic requires the "we-radar" and "we-mindset," watching for and thinking about what each team member can do or not do to help your group and your group's performance. Managing team emotions is about what team members do and say both individually and collectively.

Think of a team of 10 people. All 10 individuals have acquired ways of dealing with feelings, their own, and those of people around them. Now think of the pairs taking calls from each other or trios connecting in between team meetings. Those smaller interactions within the team, as well as when the whole team is together, offer opportunities to say and do things to help the team manage emotions well.

Managing team emotions means mobilizing the best of what feelings have to offer your group to stimulate peak team performance conditions. For example, the team that recognizes who is motivated by tight deadlines and who gets stressed out by them can more effectively request who should take the lead for a high-pressure, quick turnaround project. It also means reigning in those impulses, moods or team habits that allow a team's spirit to wane or energy to run wild and out of control. At the very least, teams need to know how to avoid mixing combustible behaviors with potentially explosive situations.

Managing team emotions is not about suppressing feelings.

The wish to kick feelings out of the room is mentioned often in employee engagement survey comments and team assessments. It typically looks and sounds like this: "People just need to leave their emotions out of it," or "People shouldn't take things so personally." This wish is understandable, as it sounds like conversations or decisions would be easier without complicated emotions, but that is not true.

The "no emotions allowed" rule is detrimental to a team because it's not physically possible. The limbic system in the brain processes emotions before thoughts and actions, so attempting to shut emotions out of a team meeting space will cut out important incoming alerts. Would you put your team members' heads in the sand as the tide rises around you? Similarly, emotions will seep into any room, physical or virtual, and into people's words and actions regardless. Every team might as well learn what managing emotions looks and sounds like, so they will know when to pull back or when to engage.

What Emotion Management Sounds Like

Accounting Team
Emotion Management score = 93

What team members say:

"During the budget process, it can get extremely emotional, and I feel we do well with helping each other through a rough time. We have a strong team where everyone supports each other 100%."

"You can see us stay on task and gain respect with each other by addressing the issue and how to resolve it, as opposed to trying to divert blame and focusing on fault."

"Participation is encouraged during weekly virtual meetings. It is a positive, supportive atmosphere. No one is personally dismissed. An idea or topic may be put out there, discussed, and then dismissed, but it's done so respectfully."

"Our team is extremely open with each other. We can honestly express our emotions, knowing there will be no judgment. Everyone provides support and, when possible, solutions. We are all ready to step in and assist without hesitation. Best team-mates ever!"

Senior Living Team
Emotion Management score = 92

What team members say:

"When roadblocks are put in our way, the team comes together to figure out an alternate route, often bringing in the source of the roadblock to help."

"I have witnessed team members with a particular viewpoint, which they strongly held around a significant issue, change their view based on the views expressed by other team members. We're somehow able to consider all issues to come to the best outcome in a situation."

"When residents have concerns, I feel we are able to sympathize and look at their perspective. When responding to their concerns, we work together to find the best solution. We also take a step back when emotions run high so we can better evaluate the situation. During those few occasions, we have managed to carefully redirect the situation to a comfortable place where the conversation can continue."

"When dealing with each other, we try to deal with the situation and not see the person as the problem."

What a Lack of Emotion Management Sounds Like

Warehouse Team
Emotion Management score = 52

What team members say:

"I wish people on my team could take the emotions out of their reactions. There are people in our group that take things so personally that they sometimes have difficulty speaking in coherent sentences because they become so flustered."

"Certain people make small issues into explosive emotional drama."

"There is little management at all. Everything is a reaction. We have an undercurrent of panic when we meet, a sense of being overwhelmed by too much to do and who's going to manage it all. Also, I feel a palpable impatience that our weekly meeting is to be endured, and everyone has more important things to do than be with each other to exchange information, make decisions, or find out how we can support each other."

"During new projects, we need to listen to the ideas of others. I don't appreciate people who go into panic mode during a crisis and expect the rest of us to show panic just because they are. Realize people show urgency differently."

Engineering Team
Emotion Management score = 56

What team members say:

"I don't think that our team as a whole manages 'negative' emotions or stress well. We don't explicitly address conflict and tension, even when it is almost palpable in the room. As a result, it festers and lowers morale in the office."

"No one speaks up when the mood is not right. Rather than choosing to discuss the topic later, we tend to struggle through the task at hand regardless of the bad mood. I've never heard any of us say, "Are we in the right mood and willing to stay on task during this discussion?"

"Sometimes during meetings, the conversation can get a little heated, especially when someone's frustrated. I think we could do a better job acknowledging this frustration and listening to people's opinions or thoughts before making a judgment or criticism."

"We have a tendency to hold in emotions, especially negative ones, and then build resentment towards someone else. It is my opinion that these resentments could be stopped if the emotions were immediately addressed and directly."

Internal Relationships

Healthy relationships among team members require time and effort to strengthen how you treat each other and work together before times get tough. Think of the team's internal relationships as an adhesive, ranging in strength. They can either act like super glue, bonding team members and holding the group together through thick and thin, or act like painter's tape, easily torn or weakened if neglected too long. When pulled under pressure, weak team relationships may not be able to hold any gains made through getting to know each other at the start.

Internal relationships are how well your team interacts with one another. It's how your team works together on good days and bad, especially during the bad days. This can feel like a big ask because each team member naturally responds to challenging situations in their own way. We've all had a lifetime of experiences that influence what we add to our team dynamic. There is rarely a one-size-fits-all team member style, so it may feel impossible to get your whole team moving in a similar direction.

To succeed, your team has to cultivate an effective team atmosphere and develop constructive work relationships among team members before the tough times arrive. Intentionally strengthening your relationships will help nurture a unique team culture that is healthy, fun, productive, and able to support your group through challenges. When your team improves your internal

> **Intentionally strengthening your relationships will help nurture a unique team culture that is healthy, fun, productive, and able to support your group through challenges.**

relationships, your members will not only consider the work to be important, but you will also value your investment in relationships as equally important teamwork.

Teams that score low on internal relationships struggle with two problems. First, team members talk about their frustrations about one teammate with another or feel worn down by observing and listening to the negative relationships within the team. These teams lack the "we-mindset." Before feeling judgmental of teams like these or embarrassed if this sounds like your team, remember that a contributing factor is that people don't know what they can do to change this unhealthy dynamic.

The other internal relationship problem is the delicate balance between productive work and feeling supported and respected as a person while working on the team. Teams with strong internal relationship skills put time and effort into getting to know one another beyond just the tasks at hand. They learn how to put positive feelings and moods to work, as well as work through difficulties with each other and the work itself.

What Internal Relationships Sound Like

Web Development Team
Internal Relationships score = 92

What team members say:

"We deal with tough situations well, like when we found that the query tool we were developing didn't meet user needs. We had to take control of the situation to get the project back on track, so as a team, we held a series of meetings almost every day for two weeks, wading through endless problems until we reached a solution that worked for everyone."

"I believe we enjoy being with each other. Each team member is very talented, and I believe that all of the members of the team recognize the value that each team member brings to the team."

"When the Q2 data was released, the tension was very high among many people in the company. All the different groups didn't know the information, and everything wasn't being passed along accurately. Everyone on my team worked together to get done what needed to be done, and through that, our relationships were stronger."

Software Sales Team
Internal Relationships score = 95

What team members say:

"The majority of us try to keep things light and humorous as much as we can to balance the stress. We don't avoid saying things when they are important, even if emotions are starting to become noticeable. We typically try to address problems in a timely manner, and almost all of us are open to suggestions and try not to take things personally."

"We have open communication with one another. If someone is going through a change personally, we all try to support one another. If there is a conflict, it is handled calmly, and usually away from others, so as to solve it privately to prevent embarrassment."

"When we pick up on a teammate that is struggling with a particular client, we always go to help that person deal with it by giving them input on why a client might feel a particular way. That way, we can all clearly understand the client and serve them properly."

"At a large offsite event, the meeting was not progressing as planned, and frustration among the attendees was rising. I'm proud of how our team was able to politely take control of the circumstance, keep time and make a significant improvement to the meeting's progress, experience, and outcome."

What a Lack of Internal Relationships Sounds Like

Recruitment Team
Internal Relationships score = 61

What team members say:

"Our team tends to complain rather than address issues. People overreact and get too concerned about things that either don't involve them or are beyond their control. I wish the team would work at keeping gossip to a minimum and mind their own business."

"I often hear comments not to help 'that' person so we can let them fall on their face. This is not a 'team' mentality, and it does not make for a pleasant environment. I don't want to see anyone fail. I want to work together."

"I fear that when we are alone in our department, we struggle to make good decisions about our attitudes, actions, and the way we relate to one another. Some of the biggest complainers are in this group, and I don't see them changing. We all need to ask ourselves, 'Am I on board?' If not, get out now."

"There are times when barbs are thrown and then covered up by joking or talking over. If we look in the mirror, we can all see that we can do better. Let's call ourselves out, admit it, apologize, and then try to not repeat it. Let's be the team that everyone aspires to be on."

AC Installation Team
Internal Relationships score = 59

What team members say:

"I don't see us forming good relationships within the team unless a few all oppose a situation. Then they band together to act against whatever the issue is."

"I would like us to get to know each other in an off-site that only builds our team emotionally and not have 'work' on the agenda."

"This team is not very social with each other or out in the organization. We are very siloed in our approach and express no interest in each other's areas unless we are in a meeting. Then we prefer email if the topic does not interest us. When people get challenged on their area of expertise, they get very defensive."

"I think our communication could be clearer when dealing with each other or trying to convey objectives. There is a risk that a lack of clarity or understanding is leading us to conflict."

"Let's work hard to eliminate behaviors that make us less effective, hurt our teammates and tarnish our reputation in the organization. Nothing good ever comes from holding a grudge."

"I think people are really good at talking behind other people's backs and triangulating, but I see a lot of reluctance to confront their feelings with the concerned parties. For those who have to listen to it, I hear them complain about it."

External Relationships

Healthy relationships with people outside the team and with other teams offer any work group additional avenues to succeed. Teams can expand their spheres of influence, find solutions and resources beyond what's available inside the team, and lend helping hands externally with the knowledge that help will return when needed. External relationships is the team EQ skill that is as much about giving as it is about taking.

Just like a person needs to look outward to improve their own relationship skills, teams must consider their relationships with people outside the team and other teams. This not only increases their team EQ skills but also widens the team's chances of meeting and exceeding their goals. Managing relationships outside the team is the group's ability to interact with other teams, individuals outside the group, the organization as a whole, and people or groups outside the company.

This is a complex skill set because even a team that works very well with each other can still come across as clueless when it comes to their interactions outside the group. Without external relationship skills, a team's hard work can go unrecognized, or worse yet, a team can ruffle feathers and find themselves creating conflicts, competition, or a negative climate around them that saps everyone's energy—theirs as well as the energy of other teams.

Managing relationships outside the team begins to redefine and expand what is meant by "we" in the team's "we-mindset." This worthwhile team EQ skill better connects every team to each other and the larger mission of the organization. Focusing on external relationships helps members of the group begin to look up and around them to consider how what they say and do helps or hinders the larger work in progress by other teams.

> **Managing relationships outside the team begins to redefine and expand what is meant by "we" in the team's "we-mindset."**

This doesn't mean your team's external relationships are just about smiling and treating outsiders nicely, though that may be part of it. Rather, it's about educating yourselves about the world you operate in and educating others about the work you do. It's recognizing when to rely on yourselves and when not to. It's also about how to take responsibility, reach out and problem solve together, and seize opportunities. This final skill ultimately connects teams throughout the organization and plays a big role in creating an emotionally intelligent organization.

What External Relationships Sound Like

Food Science Research Team
External Relationships score = 94

What team members say:

"We're making every effort as a team to establish good working relationships with the production facilities that might not always share the same willingness that we have."

"We are very supportive of each other and other teams and considerate of the needs of stakeholders."

"Our team formed good relationships working closely with other teams through communication, understanding issues, being responsive, and following up."

"As a group, I think we are good at helping each other react professionally toward other departments when emotions run high."

"Our good relationships with other departments were formed by being proactive in the way we deliver information and services to support their work."

Investment Team
External Relationships score = 90

What team members say:

"We work in a highly matrixed organization, and it would be easy for us to operate out on islands, but we work hard to avoid doing so. Even when the affiliate rules prevent us from sharing as openly as we would like, we take time to share lessons learned through our retreats and our bi-weekly update meetings."

"The group is very good at explaining our decisions to other committees within the organization at large. Any disagreement within the group at meeting time is not apparent when decisions are communicated outside the team."

"Our team collaborates with other teams that in some situations may also be our competition. Having a good relationship with them makes doing business much more pleasant and effective."

"When we're competing with the other groups, we try to understand their success and implement some of their strategies."

"I believe, as a team, we deliberate long enough to come to a decision about the right thing to do, and once that decision is made, the team supports the decision publicly in a positive manner regardless of personal opinion or preference. We offer respect to each other and to other teams whenever we encounter them in a discussion."

What a Lack of External Relationships Sounds Like

Sports Broadcasting Team
External Relationships score = 61

What team members say:

"I wish the team would realize that we need to accept other department reports and not pull them apart. They should feel like they have accomplished their job and our team appreciates its work. It is hard to be pulled apart in a public meeting."

"I don't think we understand how we are viewed by others in the organization and how we can best provide our services. Our team has a lot to offer, but we have mainly been pushing information out instead of partnering with departments."

"We should take a more collaborative approach and have realistic expectations of other departments. We need to better understand their workloads. Last week, an IT guy shared with us the expectation placed on them. It was ironic since we had passed around a comic strip that made fun of them that very day."

"Sometimes, I think our team is too confident. We need to speak in a language that other groups can relate to, so we are understood and there is buy-in. Within our own team, we need to be willing to address behaviors that reflect on our team when observed by others."

Academic Advisory Team
External Relationships score = 59

What team members say:

"Let's put ourselves in other departments' shoes and understand where they're coming from, why they are reacting the way they are, and vice versa. Communication would be better, and emotions wouldn't flare."

"Our team should take time to understand the issues raised by the department chairs rather than anticipating reactions and acting on false information. The department should also be open to constructive criticism emanating from other departments, be less defensive, and reduce the 'us and them' attitude."

"I am hoping there will be more opportunities to develop relationships with colleagues from other departments. We need a better understanding of their internal workings, and hopefully, we can provide a better understanding of our team's value to the university."

"Sometimes, the camaraderie in the open office goes a little too far. We will get caught by visitors to the office one day."

"I wish we would share more information about our projects and activities. I believe that our team is missing many opportunities for collaboration because we simply aren't aware of programs that department chairs are developing."

"We tend to be a league of teams with each competing to go to the Super Bowl. We compete to raise the most money, gain the greatest visibility, and do not always show appreciation, support, or respect for each other. We could do so much more in critical areas if we listened and supported other teams even when the subject is not our #1 interest or area of expertise."

4

—

THE PATHWAY
TO TEAM EQ:
YOUR ACTION PLAN

As you set out to increase your team EQ skills, forming new habits and breaking old ones will be on the path ahead. This path has many routes. One team might set out to build new, healthy habits, while another team might choose to extinguish a corrosive pattern. What follows is a practical approach to help your team decide what to work on as you discover team EQ strategies in the following chapters and begin to put them to good use in the work you do.

You may wonder what "rules" to follow that will help ensure you get there and get there faster. These well-known rules might be familiar to you and offer ideas about how often or how long you'll want to practice to reach your destination—exhibiting high team EQ behaviors automatically and easily. There's the *Rule of 100* (being willing to do something 100 times to get good at it), the *21/90 Rule* (practicing daily for 21 days to form the habit and then 90 more days to make the habit permanent), and the *10 Year Rule* (Ten years of learning or honing a craft to make a genius breakthrough). Don't worry about which rule is the right one, as they are each rooted in the one important approach: repeated practice.

The team EQ strategies in this book are accessible to everyone if your team uses this approach with one addition: *practice repeatedly and deliberately*. This is the basis for generating new neural connections in your brain. The *how often* and *for how long* will vary with your circumstances. If your team interrupts each other frequently, you will have multiple opportunities a day to practice letting other speakers finish before responding. If your team fails to recognize the contributions from people outside your team, you may have to wait months before a second collaborative goal is reached and you have your second chance. Research shows a considerable variation (from 18–254 days) in how long it takes a person to make a habit automatic.

Now, consider a group of people working to build habits together. It takes more time for everyone on the team to do their part in practicing. But practice. That's all. *Practice deliberately and repeatedly* is the only rule you need to remember. Your repeat practice approach will help your group mobilize your collective strength and create momentum for a habit your team has not yet acquired.

Working on your team EQ skills is not a race; it's a path you take together with intention. It requires an upfront discussion and agreement as you begin, followed by periodic check-in discussions about how things are going. Can you get started as one team member, inserting high team EQ words and actions as best you can when interacting with your team? You are certainly encouraged to model behaviors that may catch on, but you can only do your part. Some EQ strategies require all team members to do their part too.

Here's how to get started.

1. **Select one team EQ skill to work on first.** The mind can focus more effectively when not overwhelmed by too many options. One EQ skill at a time is a good start. Even motivated teams should consider that working diligently on a single skill will take you farther and move you along to the next team EQ skill faster.

2. **Choose three team EQ strategies to practice for three months.** Review the strategies available for the team EQ skill you selected and choose up to three team EQ strategies to practice. Practice these strategies for three months. You may need to continue beyond the three-month mark, but commit to three months initially for your action plan.

3. **Discuss how to go about your practice.** Keep the following in mind:

   a. **Expect progress, not perfection.** When it comes to developing new team EQ skills, waiting for perfection means you are looking to take big leaps without mistakes the first time out. That expectation won't help your team make progress. Instead, it will set you up for disappointment and frustration. Make every effort to say and do the small things that will help your team progress with small steps. Catch yourselves doing better than before, talk about what led up to this small success, and discuss what you will try next time.

   b. **Practice deliberately and repeatedly, even after setbacks.** The sheer quantity of practice isn't the only secret to increasing your team EQ skills. Often, it's your current way of doing things, your comfort zone, that holds you back. Intentionally push yourselves out of this comfort zone to say and do things differently, closer to your specific team EQ goal. As you get going, you will fall into old habits, and you may think these moments will set you back. Don't be discouraged. Setbacks are huge growth opportunities. Talk together about what led you to slip back to your old way, restate your commitment to keep going, and focus on your stated target as you practice together deliberately. Now, you have a deeper understanding of what to do next time.

c. Be patient with each other. When you work to improve your team EQ, it may take months to see observable progress and a year or two to feel mastery. Give yourselves time. Be patient with one another by pointing out the wins, however big or small. Encourage each other to keep going. Revisit the strategies chapters for finer details you may not have noticed prior to practicing.

4. **Place a monthly discussion on your team agenda.** Team EQ is likely not the typical or only topic for your team agendas, but it's a good one. Make the conversation about high team EQ moments, insights, and tips. If a strategy you select requires a more structured conversation, reread the strategy, and use the "how-to" on those pages to guide your discussion for that month.

5. **Check in on progress.** Three months from the day your team begins your team EQ journey, check in on progress. This check-in should be as simple as a question posed to the group to see if everyone feels the same way. "What progress are we making on our three team EQ strategies?" Have a

lively conversation and ask for specific examples. If you need feedback from people outside the team, seek it out.

6. **Decide together when to celebrate and move on.** Deciding to move on is similar to your progress check. "Do we all think we've made enough progress on (fill in strategy name)?" Discuss observations from each other and the feedback from people or teams outside your team about what they notice now. If you all agree the strategies in your team EQ action plan have become part of how you work together, celebrate by entering the date you completed this leg of your journey, post the completed plan somewhere with pride, and celebrate.

Each leg of your team EQ journey will be similar to the steps just described, with variations in how much time you'll have to practice in order to master the strategy. Select three more strategies and practice for three more months minimum. Be patient with each other and the team as a whole. Check in together at team meetings. A simple approach to your team EQ action plan follows.

TEAM EQ ACTION PLAN

Select One Team EQ Skill and Three Team EQ Strategies

Which of the four team emotional intelligence skills will your group work on? Check your chosen team EQ skill below:

Team EQ Skill

_____Emotion Awareness

_____Emotion Management

_____Internal Relationships

_____External Relationships

Review the strategies for the team EQ skill your group selected. Then list up to three that your group wants to practice for a minimum of three months.

Team EQ Strategies to Practice

1._____

2._____

3. _____

| Track Progress on Your Plan

Note the date your practice begins and note a date three months out to check in on your progress. Then, fill in the date your team agrees that it's time to move on to a new leg of your journey.

Dates to Track

_____Date started

_____Date to check in on progress

_____Date completed

Continue on your team EQ journey with a new action plan.

5

—

EMOTION AWARENESS STRATEGIES

In a meeting room, conference call, or email chain, your team can't see feelings swirling and surrounding the work like a cloud of dust. But they are there. Feelings enter team members' words and body language, influencing your group conversations, decisions, and relationships. By getting to know your group's moods and emotional habits, you will begin to understand how your team operates at a much deeper level than you do now. Emotion awareness strategies offer what to watch for and how to observe your group working together as you begin your team EQ journey.

The nature of awareness work is to look at and learn about your team across a wide range of situations. Your team likely responds differently in normal and stressful times, in certain and uncertain times, in cohesive and divided times, and so on. Observing for a period of time will help you notice the variety of feelings, words, and behaviors that influence your group positively and negatively. Raising your awareness also involves talking together about what the group values in each team member and how the team will access what each person has to offer.

Every team member's brain is hard-wired for emotional reactions that will surface while working together. As such, you might as well take the time to familiarize yourselves with which moods and emotions appear on your team. When a team doesn't invest the time to notice and understand the role their emotions play in their work, they give emotional dynamics the upper hand. Their feelings surface and resurface, distracting and pestering the team. Emotions will persist, and their influence will build until someone takes notice, so it's best to master the art of recognizing and understanding your team's emotions early on.

Learn to tune in to your team's emotions sooner, and they will direct your team's attention to matters of importance. You will catch yourselves ignoring potential problems to avoid negative feelings. When team members can recognize when the group is skirting an issue or ignoring some voices, they can move team discussions in a more inclusive direction earlier.

Getting in touch with your team's emotions and habits takes

time and a willingness to risk talking about how each of you feel individually and together. Be patient and give yourselves credit for small steps forward. When you begin to notice things separately or collectively about how the team behaves (things you had no idea about before), you are progressing.

This chapter introduces you to 11 team EQ strategies for emotion awareness. Each strategy will help your group proactively learn about each other and better understand the cloud of feelings that swirls up into your team workspace. They are designed to help you build a solid foundation for understanding how you work together. The strategies are easy to put into action and packed with team EQ insights and examples that will help your group grow together over time.

EMOTION AWARENESS STRATEGIES

1.   Understand One Another
2.   Check in on One Another
3.   Notice and Acknowledge Discomfort
4.   Catch the Mood in the Room
5.   Surface the Quieter Feelings
6.   Recognize Your Team's Triggers
7.   Find the Source of Your Team's Emotions
8.   Be Thoughtful, Whether Divided or United
9.   Get to Know Your Team under Stress
10. Learn from Your Team's EQ Mistakes
11. Visit Your Team's Values

1 Understand One Another

There are so many things to learn about your fellow team members to really understand one another. Who's a morning bird or a night owl? Are you a texter or an emailer? Who likes caffeine, salt, or candy to help push through those long days? These are all valuable and fun tidbits. The target for a higher team EQ also includes understanding each other's emotional patterns and the influences they have within the group.

We all experience emotions dozens of times each day, and over weeks, months, and years we form emotional habits, meaning we respond to certain situations in reliable ways. Think of these feeling patterns as threads woven into the fabric of your team's story. They can either help you achieve great things together or cause you to stumble over each other again and again. If, as a team, you can notice and understand the role that team member emotions play within the group, the mystery behind them dissolves, and they won't get in your way.

So, how can you practice this strategy as a team? In a group setting, ask yourselves a few questions. This first question is the overarching goal of the discussion: "What is the role that our emotions play in our work and our team interactions?" The way to arrive at the answer is to discuss this second two-part question: "What is one tendency you have for a specific emotion that gets in your way? And how do your teammates react when this happens?" The key is to consider specific moments and behaviors as examples.

You can get as formal (think whiteboarding the example below for your own team) or casual (think conversation, minus the note-taking) as you want. It might take some time or a few meetings to map this out. If you have new team members, there is no need to require a response, but encourage one. By the end, this conversation will allow your team to picture your current team EQ dynamic, figuratively or literally. For example, here's a fictional team of four made up of Esteban, Annie, Cecilia, and Bob.

When I feel this way, I tend to:	Team reactions to this tendency
I (Bob) shut down when I'm frustrated.	Esteban shuts down too. Cecilia gets fired up when Bob does that! Annie feels for Bob and defends him.
I (Esteban) sweep tough moments under the rug. Best to go on with the day.	Cecilia gets fired up over this, too. Annie speaks up for Esteban. Bob feels relief that Esteban doesn't want to get into it.
I (Cecilia) talk too much when I'm overwhelmed and will talk to anyone who will listen.	Bob does not pick up the phone when Cecilia's in this state. Esteban listens but feels drained afterward. Annie listens and feels helpful for listening.
I (Annie) put others first when I'm stressed instead of taking care of myself.	Bob gets frustrated—he's seen this before. Esteban encourages Annie to consider herself. Cecilia listens and feels helpful for listening.

With this new information before you, discuss your insights as a team. Talk through your emotions and reactions and how your new awareness will benefit your group. You can only manage what you're aware of, and after this conversation, your team emotions will hold less power over the flow of work. It's nearly impossible to learn every emotional tendency across every situation for every member of your team, but this exercise is powerful because it reveals a way to understand and respond to each other's emotions more deliberately.

2 Check in on One Another

Diving in a frigid kelp forest near Cape Town, South Africa, Craig Foster encountered an octopus—a notably antisocial and highly intelligent animal that is a master of camouflage and pattern recognition. The octopus was characteristically skittish and retreated each day as Foster approached. After months of daily visits, she recognized his presence, and the boundaries between Foster and the normally isolated sea creature began to dissolve. Foster's regular underwater check-ins built trust between them as he learned about her home, defenses, and curiosity. In time, she sought Foster out and even extended her arm to initiate physical contact, an unheard-of vulnerability for this species with a large variety of predators.

This rare relationship between Craig and an octopus only became possible because Foster checked in on the octopus regularly and in a comfortable, non-intrusive way. While, of course, teammates are not skittish octopi, Foster's approach offers some guiding principles for checking in with teammates. Your team can build trust, develop comfort with each other, and learn to read one another with greater accuracy by checking in frequently with respect and genuine care. For example, little things, such as hearing that cousins with a baby are visiting your teammate's house, may explain her being on mute during a virtual team meeting. She is managing background noise, not disengaging. Taking the time to check in and learn these kinds of little things can help your team cooperate more smoothly. Even the most reticent of your teammates may engage when you create a specific time and a comfortable, safe space where everyone has complete choice about what to share. However you design and approach your check-ins, they can help you connect and become more astute about what's really going on with one another.

A more formal type of check-in can be scheduled and facilitated by the team leader or a teammate. The facilitator moves from person to person, balances time, and encourages sharing without requiring it. Done weekly, a check-in of about 10 minutes allows team members to share how they are feeling that day or week. Done monthly or quarterly, a longer check-in of about 30 minutes may encourage people to share their life's milestones or challenges. This is the time to simply listen and learn from your teammates. It may even be worth establishing a few ground rules (i.e., there are no good or bad emotions) so your check-ins result in connection, not alienation.

A less formal check-in, done on the fly and as needed, allows your teammates to understand and take care of each other. For example, you may notice a team member who is tired or not their usual self. Find a moment to ask how they are doing or how their work is going. Just as Foster recognized behavior changes when the octopus coped with injuries and moved through phases of her life, you may recognize differences in a teammate's demeanor over time. Asking how "things are going" might reveal how you or the team can offer more support.

Foster explained that his check-ins with the octopus taught him "to become sensitized to the other." Likewise, your team check-ins will help you become sensitized to each other too. Check-ins offer intangible threads that will bond your team and make emotions a normal part of your work together.

3 Notice and Acknowledge Discomfort

Let's face it. We can't actually hear what's going on in someone else's head. So how is it that we can still sense when a team member is uncomfortable, disappointed, rejected, or resistant?

We began learning this as kids during recess, at the park, or in gym class when we lined up for picking teams. When the last kid stood isolated, fiercely casual, and avoiding eye contact, everyone knew that kid felt mortified. Yet, we also felt relief that it wasn't us and that the pain of the moment would be over soon. Our brains were already wired to sense and feel beyond their body movements and facial expressions that tried to mask internal anguish, wishes to flee, or reluctance to join.

What you didn't learn back then was how important it is to show your team members that you notice their discomfort and acknowledge it. Signs of discomfort are valuable bits of information. They can be early warning signs to factors not considered, a tip-off that someone is struggling, or an early example of how people outside your team might react. When discomfort is acknowledged, the team is in a better position to see the whole picture, attend to unfinished business, support a hurting teammate, and help everyone perform at their best. Make it clear that negative feelings and reactions are valid and important and that the team wants to understand. Ask questions and listen actively. Maybe add, "Thanks for describing how it makes you feel." Acknowledging them doesn't mean you have to act on those feelings. You're just giving time and space to hear and understand them. That's all.

4 **Catch the Mood in the Room**

You could hear a pin drop as the producer walked out of the theater after telling the cast that ticket sales were low. Their long-running Off Broadway play was in jeopardy of closing. After about two minutes of heavy silence, the understudy David blurted out the lead role's climactic line, "Well, that's unfortunate!" The whole group laughed and then began to share how devastated they felt at the thought of losing their show after so much hard work.

Sometimes that's all it takes when your team becomes uncomfortable, resistant, reactive, or carried away. One team member can step back, notice that everyone is struggling, and then break the ice by acknowledging the atmosphere. Catching the mood in the room adds to everyone's understanding of the moment and enables your group to talk through how you feel so you can begin to allow it to subside.

The first step to this strategy is to experience the mood yourself. Emotions are catchy, spreading from person to person. By taking notice of what you're feeling, you will often catch the palpable vibe around you as well. Another easy way to go about this is to observe the people around you. When David was in the theatre, he could surely look around and see dismayed or distracted faces (furrowed brows, gazing off into the distance, even tears), defeated body language (slumped shoulders, heads down or in hands), and hear the silence (a tangible weight in the room).

After you recognize the mood in the room, the second step is to call it out. Many people quit at this step because they're uncomfortable interrupting the group or they're not sure how to do so without upsetting people. What worked so well in David's case was that instead of worrying too much about getting it exactly right, he picked up on the general feeling around him and then commented in a way he knew his team would appreciate. You can't worry too much about getting the label perfect because emotions in a room vary slightly from person to person and mix to create the overall mood.

When you catch and name the mood in the room, you give your team the opportunity to talk about it and move away from siloed rumination. This lays the groundwork for managing team emotions together because they have to be understood in order to be managed. Catching the mood in the room offers one more benefit. It makes it normal to discuss emotions with each other instead of adopting a "there's no place for emotions in our teamwork" mentality.

5 Surface the Quieter Feelings

Lake Volta is the largest manmade reservoir in the world. The lake is contained behind the Akosombo Dam, which generates a substantial amount of electricity for the people of Ghana. If only a portion of Lake Volta were sectioned off to power the dam, the resulting electricity would amount to a fraction of Akosombo's potential, and many in Ghana would be left without this major source of power. Not the best use of this natural resource's unique potential.

The same thing happens when you tap only some of the voices at your table. When only a few members on your team contribute, the resulting creativity, insights, or critical analysis is at best only a portion of what's possible. Be attentive about who on the team speaks up and who doesn't. Don't allow a couple members of your group to speak on behalf of everyone's feelings.

Quieter team members and those who were absent must also be heard. Their feelings and reactions are that valuable, untapped resource. Encourage the quieter feelings on the team to surface by checking in with the quiet ones. When you notice that a team member has not spoken in a meeting, ask the person on behalf of the team, "How do you feel about what is being discussed?" Be patient. If the person is not sure in the moment, give them space to reflect and suggest a time to revisit how all team members feel about the topic at hand. Often, quiet members are quiet because they process thoughts and feelings internally over time as opposed to talkative people, who tend to process thoughts and feelings out loud through conversation. Likewise, if a team member is absent, fill them in later and ask their take on the matter.

When your team pays close attention to all its members, you tap into a deeper resource well. Just as the resources of Lake Volta are tapped for maximum electricity output, diverse feelings and reactions on the team are needed to fully power your team's potential.

6 Recognize Your Team's Triggers

In baseball, a curveball is difficult to hit for two reasons. First, a curveball travels slower than usual, messing up the timing of a batter's swing. Second, a curveball changes direction, or "curves," mid-air, messing up the direction of a batter's swing. When batters are caught off guard by a curveball, it's usually because they missed the pitch's signature spin. The result is an awkward swing ahead of the ball's curving arc. Even the most talented baseball players can be extremely frustrated by a well-thrown curveball.

Curveballs catch teams off guard too. When something surprising is "thrown" in your team's direction, it can ignite a big reaction. Your team thinks it's facing one thing, but it's really facing something else entirely. This can trigger team members and cause your team to become distracted, moody, reactive, or unproductive. What helps to successfully manage your team's triggers is to first recognize their signs. To crush a curveball, the batter spots the different spin right out of the pitcher's hand, signaling the arrival delay and the ball's sharp trajectory change. Similarly, your team can pinpoint the types of people (like doubters), situations (like feeling caught off guard), or conditions (like noisy offices) that trigger strong emotions or poor performance.

When your team is triggered, you all have to be prepared to spot the unexpected and deal with it effectively then and there. Set aside time, perhaps in a reoccurring team meeting, to discuss what situations, behaviors, or conditions have caused unwanted strong reactions over the past month. This can help identify future curveballs that might come your way again.

Seek to learn more about how team members typically respond and behave in these impactful situations. Do they withdraw? Do they vent? Do they become distracted? Or do some buckle down and get more focused? Encourage people to share examples of what triggers them and discuss how the resulting reactions affect your teamwork.

Curveballs happen now and again and so do emotional triggers. A batter who spots a curveball can adjust their swing quickly. Likewise, the team that can spot their triggers can also adjust their response sooner. This allows them to take control of their emotional reaction before it has the chance to escalate and negatively impact their performance or their relationships.

7 Find the Source of Your Team's Emotions

To get a sense of how complex your team's emotions are, picture how geologists study glaciers. On the surface, they can observe the weather's impact at that moment in time. As they drill into the ice and pull out the core, they begin to see patterns through history in temperature, precipitation, volcanic activity, and wind. Your team's emotions run deep too, whether it's one person, several people, or the whole team. Emotional team members feel the way they do for a reason. A closer look will often reveal critical issues like crossed boundaries, dashed hopes, touched nerves, changing needs, and high-pressure situations.

Here's what you can do to drill deeper. Next time you spot your teammate in an emotional moment, don't just chalk it up to an "off day." Linger for a moment to learn more. One of the most powerful ways to seek the source of your team's emotions is to wonder why. Let's say, as an example, you notice your teammate James rolling his eyes, crossing his arms, and not contributing. Perhaps James' behavior stands out because you know he's normally outgoing and energized by group brainstorms. You might wonder, "Why is James acting differently this time?" It could be that the topic at hand is his pet project of fourteen months, and other people are jumping to different conclusions about things he's already put a year's worth of deliberation into. It could be that all the recent changes in the organization and your team's leadership are catching up to him (and likely to other members too in that case). It could be that he's overloaded with work and his teammates need to step in to help him out. It could be something personal. The point is that context matters. Taking the time to be genuinely interested and to empathize with James may be all that's required of your team to understand where he's coming from and how his reaction fits into the team's work or next steps.

Other times, you need to look deeper. You might say, "I noticed you've been a bit quieter than usual, is everything alright?" James may not reveal all the information you wish for right then, but this question gives him the chance to share. It also shows him that your team notices and cares about how he's feeling, where he's coming from, and what he's thinking.

Think of this initial question or comment as a kind of foot-in-the-door moment. The goal isn't to get James to unravel his childhood. Instead, the goal is to remain open and curious about how he's feeling, to make it clear you want to understand where he's coming from, and to show you care about him as a person. If digging even deeper is needed, it may be necessary for the leader or someone close to James to seek a one-on-one conversation.

Often, it's not just one teammate who is feeling a certain way in response to what's going on. A few or even the whole team may feel emotions they don't completely understand. Begin your exploration by looking at your own feelings as a way to drill deeper as a group. Share and then ask a question such as "I've been feeling overwhelmed lately. Has anyone else been feeling this way too?"

Many teams have to move quickly to accomplish everything on their plates. To save time, emotions in all their discomfort and complexity are dealt with on only a surface level—the team responding only to what is shared directly. As you start to think of drilling deeper to the source of feelings as an opportunity to deepen your team's awareness, your perspective on "lost time" will change. Drilling deeper will lead you to increased efficiency, trust, and cohesion when it really matters.

8 Be Thoughtful, Whether Divided or United

One of the fastest ways to temporarily blind your team to potential problems or possibilities is to become overly divided or united. That's because the emotions take over, and thoughtful conversations get pushed to the side.

Division usually begins with good intentions. Consider a marketing campaign launch with a tight deadline. One team member is sure it should allocate funds to T.V. commercials, and one teammate agrees. Then, a couple other people advocate that "T.V. is old-school and the money would be better allocated for social media." Both sides are passionate about their perspectives and want the team to succeed. As they defend their viewpoints, people butt heads, emotions escalate, and in time, their emotions not only take over the conversation but also follow-up emails and meetings. The ongoing back and forth unwinds into "yes versus no" thinking. Now the team is vulnerable to losing sight of the goal and may lose sight of how they're treating each other. People get defensive, aggressive, personal, and overly opinionated, while others feel outcast or uncomfortable sharing a different perspective.

When you catch your team moving down this path, know that it's not a good time to sit back and let the argument resolve itself, and it's definitely not a good time to make final decisions. Instead, focus on lifting up and out as a group to see beyond the point of disagreement. Call the divide to everyone's attention and encourage alternate perspectives and ideas beyond the few that you're stuck on. Collaborating will redirect people's attention toward the bigger goal.

United teams also cut themselves off from the bigger picture. It's hard to believe, but this happens. Someone senior on a united team pitches an idea for a video campaign, and everyone immediately and unanimously jumps on board. The idea is half-baked, but instead of digging deeper, the whole team says "yes" and rides the excitement of the new idea. One reason we gravitate toward consensus like this is that it feels great—at least initially. We all like to be on teams that act cohesively and enthusiastically. It's also uncomfortable to be the person who points out a problem when no one else does.

Treat hasty agreement as a sign that other perspectives and feelings aren't finding their way into the light. Notice this moment and point it out to the group. Your next step is to slow down, linger on the idea, and ask more questions. If you need to, schedule a second session for this very purpose. Consider assigning team members to opposing or alternate viewpoints just to move perspective and thoughtful considerations back into your direct line of sight.

9 Get to Know Your Team under Stress

After a major error attempting a two-and-a-half twist vault, Simone Biles—proclaimed the greatest gymnast ever—withdrew from the 2021 Tokyo Olympic team competition, the all-around competition, and most individual events for which she qualified. Biles cited extreme stress and a dangerous condition known as the "twisties," where your body and mind are so out of sync that you lose your bearings on your body's relationship to the ground. Simone felt it best that she let the rest of the team step in rather than risk severe injury. Fans lauded Biles for extreme self-awareness, while critics blasted her for being a quitter. Everyone, however, focused largely on her as an individual.

The more interesting story is the team dynamic and how they responded under stress on the world stage. What happened instead of feeling abandoned by Biles was a shift in the roles on the team. Biles became the motivator and adjunct coach, while her teammates stepped up to compete in more events and win team, all-around, and individual event medals. Would they have won more medals with Biles competing? Certainly not if Biles lost her bearings, or even worse, injured herself.

Ideally, all your team members are healthy and performing

at their best, but that is never a given. Before your team encounters major stress, ask yourselves this important question, "What happens to us as a team when stress arises?" Discussing this question proactively will help you perform better when stress enters your team's space. Your group will become very familiar with your own emotional "twisties," signs that your team is so out of sync that you're losing your bearings and relationship to the work. As you would for a natural disaster like a fire, earthquake, or tornado, prepare a disaster plan ahead of time. Elite athletes who train, travel, eat, and live together intuitively learn how their team will handle difficulties. The rest of us need to make more of a concerted effort.

In a moment of calm, talk together about how the team has responded to stress in the past, both positively and negatively. Use one ground rule: Say "we" rather than "I" or "you." Brainstorm a list and then discuss. Consider these questions and topics:

1. What does daily stress look and sound like in our teamwork? What about major stress?

2. How and when have we buckled under stress?

3. How and when have we handled stress well?

4. How does stress influence…
   - Our decision-making?

   - Our confidence?

   - Our communication? Consider in-person, phone, virtual, chat rooms, and email.

   - Our results, goals, and performance?

   - How we treat each other?

   - How we treat people outside of our team?

Once you describe your team under stress, what will be your disaster plan when major stress takes over? Narrow your plan down to a couple things to try next time.

In Tokyo, Biles and her gymnastics team knew how to adjust to stress and support each other as one team member escaped disaster and others stepped up. Similarly, teams that are emotionally aware and prepared can flex under stress and support each other to achieve the best results possible.

10 Learn from Your Team's EQ Mistakes

The first time Maria, now a public relations executive, heard the phrase "post-mortem" was at her first job out of college. She was in the junior seat on a public relations team with a bunch of smart superstars who rarely made mistakes. Then something went seriously wrong with a project. The next morning, she saw an email announcing that they were going to have a post-mortem. *Um, sorry?* Funny how years later she would share with her staff, "I don't even remember the mistake itself, but I will never forget seeing "post-mortem" in my inbox. I'd never taken Latin, but I knew that phrase had something to do with death." She thought, *Yikes. Was I being fired? Were we being fired?*

No one was fired. In this post-mortem, she entered a room with the whole team, from vice presidents to assistants, and the whole room was free from blame. It was this team's time to look at what worked and what didn't work. It was also an opportunity to decide how to handle things next time. No dead bodies. No firing. Just learning from mistakes together to see things they didn't see in the moment. Think of it like a football team on Monday pressing pause on a replay to study where and how they lost in the final play of the game.

For a team EQ mistake, picture a post-mortem with

emotions included in the agenda. Have this meeting once the dust has settled on a significant team mistake, but soon enough that the memories and feelings are still fresh (within a month after the mistake). Remind yourselves that emotions leading up to your mistake could be contributors and make them part of your post-mortem analysis. Allow each team member to share what worked and what didn't work. Include thoughts and feelings that were at play, past and present. Talk about what to do differently next time.

Post-mortems can breathe new life (pun intended) into your future teamwork. The mistake can now morph into an opportunity for the team to learn from and about one another. This, in turn, will bring you closer, increase accountability, raise your awareness, and deepen understanding.

11 **Visit Your Team's Values**

When your team is out of sync and performance is declining, you may watch accountability and productivity disappear while relationships and the work suffer. During moments like these, there's a tendency for teams to lose their way further by jumping in to problem solve the suffering work. A better first step may be to pause and revisit your team's values. Are recent team behaviors contrary to the core beliefs you thought your team lived by?

Team values are your group's compass, your method of finding true north for working together and getting back on track when you veer. They are a set of beliefs that can guide your behavior and your decisions. A published set of team values is a great way to build alignment, camaraderie, and clarity about the path you're taking together. An example of a team value might be "respect" or "risk-taking." If respect is a declared value, your team will be highly attentive to taking time to listen deeply to one another and value each other's opinions. If risk-taking is a value, your team will be receptive to long-shot, unusual ideas and value the learning moments that result when things fail or don't go according to plan.

To find the set of values that will guide your group, ask yourselves this simple question, "What are the most important and necessary values by which we wish to work together?" List them, distribute them, and post them where you meet together. Capture congruent and incongruent behaviors that demonstrate what each value looks like in action or when violated. If "integrity" is a team value, a congruent behavior might include "we give credit where credit is due," and an incongruent behavior might be "we are not transparent in our communications."

Like a compass, team values are useless if you don't take them out to consult now and then. Soon the team will disregard or forget this invaluable team EQ tool. To keep values in working order, include them on team meeting agendas, so they are never far from view. Weave them into your discussions, praising team members who reflect a team value in action, and consult your values list together before entering a challenging conversation or making a difficult decision. Visiting your team values regularly ensures they become part of each team member's muscle memory, activated before the team behaves in ways contrary to what you had agreed to.

Team values are intended to endure and guide you along many journeys together, but environments do change. At some point, as you return to your values, you may realize that adjusting one makes total sense. Ask yourselves, "Are there any others that aren't as relevant and should be replaced?" There may be a new north star that should be added.

6

—

EMOTION MANAGEMENT STRATEGIES

Emotion management strategies give you and your team the ability to navigate emotional ebbs and flows that push or pull your team toward success or disaster. It's a back-and-forth repeated over and over—reading emotions accurately and then reacting in ways that are beneficial to the team's work, the team's internal and external relationships, and the goals of the organization.

Strategies for managing team emotions aren't about learning to stuff feelings away or ignore the mood in the room. They are about responding effectively to the range of emotional situations that surface during good times and bad. The goal is to learn how to get out of your own way, how to react nimbly to change, and how to mobilize a kind of momentum that requires intuitive, agile interactions. You and your teammates will use what you see and hear to decide what the next best move is: what to say or do; what not to say or do; to stop; to slow down; to move ahead; or to rise to the challenge.

One person on a team can make all the difference in moments that scream out for emotion management. Imagine these simple statements: "Wait, let's hear her out," "Maybe we should take a break from this," "What if we devote some extra time to this?" or "Who could give us more perspective?" That's the beauty of team EQ skills. They don't usually require the entire team to know what to do, nor do they require that the team leader shoulder all the responsibility. All it takes is one person to notice a need and say the right thing to help the team avoid being swept away by an emotional current.

The remainder of this chapter provides you with 14 specific emotion management strategies to help you and your team before and during moments that have the potential to escalate or erode team bonds. Begin by establishing effective group norms. Norms lighten the load on everyone's mind about what is expected of each person on the team. From there, these strategies will help you and your group understand how to share the energy of positive emotions. The strategies will also help you reign in the destructive power of negative emotions and learn from them. You will discover what to say and do in those moments and learn to respond to team difficulties in healthier ways.

EMOTION MANAGEMENT STRATEGIES

1. Set Norms and Enforce Them Lightly
2. Focus on Healthy Reactions to Change
3. Find and Spread Positivity
4. Hear People Out
5. Step Back
6. Take a Break
7. Go Ahead and Vent, Briefly and with Purpose
8. Seek Outside Perspective
9. Set Aside Time for Problem-Solving
10. Make Better Use of Team Time
11. When Emotions Run High, Rethink Your Team's Approach
12. Follow Through on Team Commitments
13. Strive to Make the Most of a Bad Situation
14. Give Grief Its Time and Space

Emotion
Management
Strategies

1 **Set Norms and Enforce Them Lightly**

When Google's People Analytics division set out to study team success, they expected to discover the perfect mix of personalities, backgrounds, and motivations. Instead, after more than a year studying 100+ teams at work, the only pattern they found was that high-performing teams had norms that guided how team members treated each other. Interestingly, there were no patterns among the norms either. What worked for one team was the exact opposite of what worked for another team.

Norms are the ground rules that your team will agree to and adhere to most of the time. They include standards for behavior, traditions for team successes, and agreements for how you interact. They encourage participation for the team's sake and will typically override any one team member's personal preferences. For example, starting meetings right on time or chatting for the first 5 minutes are each equally viable team norms. Team norms take the guesswork out of working together. They raise group awareness around expectations and give people permission to hold each other accountable.

If you are selecting norms for the first time, revisiting them as you welcome a new hire, or evaluating whether they still make sense after several years, you want your norms to fit three contexts: Your group, your work, and your organization's culture. In other words, it's a matter of knowing your members and the challenges ahead and selecting your norms accordingly. Here are three ways to set and refresh team norms.

1. Start with a blank slate and brainstorm a list together.
2. Ask a few team members to compile a list that the team votes on.
3. Search online for lists of norms and bring your favorites to a team meeting for review.

Then, work through the list by discussing each one. However you approach it, the goal is to select a reasonable number, about 5–10 norms.

Now and then, someone will ignore or break from your norms, and this isn't cause for major concern. They are simply voting against a norm with their actions rather than their words. This could be intentional but more likely unintentional. That said, your team doesn't want to look the other way either, or your efforts to establish norms will feel like a waste of time. You'll find people are less likely to respond negatively when norms are enforced lightly. "Hey, Lance. Does our meeting time still work for you? Or would it help if we changed it by 30 minutes, so you're able to join us at the start?" Or make it funny by shuffling as a group over to Lance's office and announcing his escort to the meeting. These gestures avoid punishing Lance and let him know that the norm, "meetings need everyone there," still stands. Define for yourselves what a friendly reminder looks and sounds like, and be open to revisiting the norms when team member actions suggest a norm isn't standing.

2 Focus on Healthy Reactions to Change

In the face of a big, unwieldy change, having an open conversation about your team's reaction might seem too late. But, as time passes, ever-widening gaps can grow between team members' reactions to change, unraveling your team's productivity and well-being when you need it most. Here are four instinctual reactions to change and how they can turn unhealthy over time. Notice that negative feelings about change reflect the mind's assessment that change is a potential threat.

Feelings about Change	Unhealthy Reactions
Lost and confused. What just happened?	Wasted energy attempting to figure out what to do. Become unnecessarily detail-oriented. Appear to need a great deal of guidance and leave work untouched until all questions have been answered.
Threatened, vulnerable, worried, or sad. Is this change a threat?	Mentally and emotionally absent, but physically present. Energies are still assessing the change and clinging to old procedures for security.
Fearful. This change is definitely a threat.	Withdrawn or disengaged. Being hard to find or doing only enough to get the job done. Lost initiative and interest.
Angry or mad. The past is gone.	Negativity or enlisting support of others. Forming coalitions and bad-mouthing.

Focusing on a healthy reaction to change is a balancing act that your team can attempt together. Give each other the chance to acknowledge that no one can change those things that are now different, and it is expected for people to have feelings about it. Also, give each other the chance to express their feelings about the change.

Then discuss this important shift in your group's thinking: Your team can begin to take control over your reactions. The following methods will help your group listen carefully and engage with each person's experience.

For those feeling confused or lost, it helps them to hear the ways that their roles and work fit into the change. They may also respond well to a series of steps to work on. This removes ambiguity and offers the guidance their feelings seek.

For those feeling threatened or vulnerable, help them understand that work and emotion can be separated. When they see their work is no longer the same, they mistakenly think their positive feelings about their team will also never be the same. Help them to identify what they liked before the change, to anticipate letting go of the old ways, and to explore ways of finding or creating similar positive feelings in new ways.

For those who don't seem present, draw them out so they can talk about their concerns. Listening and offering empathy or support can lead to a productive discussion that helps lessen their fears.

For those feeling angry, help move them from a highly negative state to a more neutral state by allowing them to let off steam. When you acknowledge that their anger is normal, and you don't hold it against them, they get the chance to make peace with it. Sometimes anger masks one of the other reactions and must be released before your teammate can find their underlying reaction.

Once feelings are acknowledged and expressed, then explore together how to frame your circumstance in a forward-moving direction (e.g., selling the office building saves rent and confirms our team will be working remotely). This is the best way to find realistic, healthy reactions and to establish your next actions. You don't have to be fake and pretend everything feels fine or easy. It helps to discuss this useful question together: "Now that we understand how everyone is feeling about this change, what are some of the things we should be doing next?"

Your team now understands the emotional baggage change can bring. Set aside time to unpack what your team is feeling to make sure emotions don't get suppressed or overlooked. Also, try to talk about how the team is reacting so you all can better frame your next steps in a healthy way. Then, you can get on with your work, having at least addressed the added emotional weight. Gradually, those seemingly intangible qualities discussed at your organization—adaptability, flexibility, resilience, and agility—begin to describe the healthy ways your team responds to change.

3 **Find and Spread Positivity**

The classic question "Is this glass half full or half empty?" is meant to show whether you hold a positive or negative outlook. The problem with the question is that it forces you to choose one, concluding that your state of mind is permanently fixed. Try saying the question as a statement: This glass is half full and half empty. Both are true, and this is closer to how teamwork can be described. Different team members can feel positive and negative at the same time. It's important to acknowledge that both can influence a team's dynamic and have consequences for the group. So, the question to ask yourselves is this: Which feelings will better help us achieve what we set out to do? Most of the time, the answer is to find and spread positivity.

Remember that mirror neurons reside across wide areas of our brain and serve as a kind of social awareness Wi-Fi, allowing us to remotely plug into the feelings of the people around us. There's even one type of mirror neuron whose sole purpose is to detect smiles and laughter, stimulating return smiles and laughter. It's because of mirror neurons that our positive emotions are quite literally contagious, spreading from member to member.

Teammates who are feeling enthusiastic and optimistic will have a visceral effect on everyone else, especially when their positive feelings are rooted in reality. So, tap those peppy people to share their points of view, send out good news over email, or laugh out loud in the halls, especially when the group needs to get up and go. Your positive teammates can serve up their belief in the team's capabilities when others need it. In the face of change, they can keep your team hopeful by spelling out the things that will change for the better and the ways your team will emerge more cohesive and productive on the other side.

Think of finding your team's positivity as a small group of joggers trying to maintain an even pace. Any one jogger will naturally experience stronger and weaker phases during their run. During a weak-feeling phase, the strengths of others in the running group will help that jogger push forward without slowing down. Positive emotions within your team will offer the same kind of flow to the natural ebbs a few may feel. Team members can draw strength from different members at different times to maximize the group's positivity. This will help your team maintain momentum.

Now your team can relax about having those varied states of mind, from the glass being half full on "good" days to seeming like it's half empty on "lousy" days. No one has to carry the pressure of being all positive all the time. Instead, your team will balance and carry each other.

4 Hear People Out

It takes courage to share how you feel, especially in front of a group. That's why when someone on your team speaks up during an important or difficult conversation, one of the worst things you can do as a team is to cut them off or make them feel unheard.

Brief moments where your team rolls past someone's perspective may seem like a small mistake (especially in fast-paced environments where moving on quickly is normal). However, they can have lingering repercussions for your team. Failing to hear people out contributes to a team culture of "emotions have no place here" or "not everyone's opinion matters equally."

Hearing people out can be as simple as someone stepping in to say, "Hey, let's hear them out. I don't think they're finished." It can also be a more formal team norm that's built into the very fabric of how your team communicates. For example, at Toyota manufacturing plants, they place a cord in the assembly line for anyone to pull at any time to stop the line for safety, errors, or broken parts.

While team conversations don't have pullable cords when emotions surface, they can still benefit from this analogy. First, by letting anyone pull the cord, Toyota empowers the assembly team from bottom to top, sending the message that each team member's eyes and ears matter. Second, letting anyone pull the cord sends the message that everyone is equally accountable. If you have the power to pull the cord and you don't, you're accountable too. The same goes for slowing the pace of a team discussion to let each person finish speaking uninterrupted. Making it important to hear people out creates a two-way street where the team is accountable for listening and each team member for speaking.

During a difficult conversation, be patient and let each person share how they feel before changing the direction of the meeting. You will find this sometimes includes posing follow-up questions to understand where they're coming from. Your team may want to let people get their feelings out first so they can then find the words to express the "why" behind their perspective. Remember that the way your team approaches the emotions of its members sends a message to everyone. Hear people out, or you might not hear from anyone.

5 **Step Back**

Taking a step back as a team can be tough to practice, especially when you are knee-deep in the muck of a situation. Grappling with a problem, tackling conflicting or shifting priorities, and searching for order without clarity or direction are all in the "muck" that holds you in place. When your team steps back and out from all the muck, you can view the moment from further away with a clearer perspective. Some might view this as walking away or even quitting. Not so! A conscious step back allows you to look at what you are facing, as if through the objective eyes of a third party.

Health care professionals use a head-to-toe assessment as a methodical outside look at their patient's major body systems. This is a checklist of sorts that directs the professional to start at the top of the skull, continue through the mid-section of the body, and finish at the feet. The checklist is especially necessary when a patient is distracted with pain and stress or can't explain what they're feeling.

When your team members are distracted with pain or can't explain what they are feeling, it is possible for your team to assess objectively, as a nurse or doctor would. Here's what you can try. First, the team needs to agree to step back for an outside-looking-in discussion of the situation. Second, decide who on your team can serve as the team's "objective third party." This person typically stays calm under pressure and can stick to a plan (or checklist) when times get tough. You can select one person or rotate roles, but have a plan. Third, as a team, adapt this healthcare head-to-toe assessment concept to your work, create a checklist that will help you maintain objectivity, and assess the situation completely. Like a head-to-assessment, the list should keep you on track and ensure you cover everything you need to.

Consider what your team needs to be healthy and in working order and create a list. The list can include both project-specific items as well as teamwork types of things. If you want to be literal, think about what you would list at the top (the head, eyes, shoulders) and so on. Instead of body parts, your list could have timelines, milestones, decision points, ways to communicate, and norms. This is how you distance your group from emotions that will otherwise get in the way. You also don't have to follow this list. You could create your own list of what your team looks like when it's "unhealthy" or something else entirely. If you want to troubleshoot together, ask your assigned, objective person to describe the situation out loud in the third-person, followed by a question to the group—"This is a team that is facing [such and such]. What should the team do next to get the best results?"

Below is a sample checklist of a team that assessed how they operate when they're "healthy."

Our Head-to-Toe Team Health Assessment

☑ Roles: clear, and there's no role confusion

☑ Communication: timely, the right people included, clear

☑ Process: steps understood, smooth hand-offs, gets results

☑ Resources: support the work, not wasted, don't slow results

☑ Emotions: allowed to inform us, managed constructively

When your list is drafted, review it together and test if it accomplishes two things: First, does it help the team see things objectively from an outsider's perspective? Second, does it lead to a discussion about achieving the results you need to achieve? Taking this step back together with the third-person perspective can break your team out of the day-to-day routine and challenge everyone to think, see, and feel the issue in a different, more effective way.

6 Take a Break

If you've ever witnessed a fistfight, the combatants hopefully had smart friends nearby who instinctively tried to pull the two apart and demanded that they take some space to catch their breath and cool down. Thankfully, we don't witness many fistfights in our teamwork, but we do witness and participate in emotionally charged moments that inhibit effective collaboration. So when outrage, panic, defeat, passion, and other intense emotions overtake your team, mimic those savvy friends and call for a break.

You might say, "Things are getting heated here. I'd feel better if we could take a break, collect our thoughts, and then figure out how to proceed. Let's not make things worse." If your group's mood is escalating quickly, people may not notice or heed your suggestion right away. Expect that some people in the room won't even hear you the first time. Say it again, using an arm wave if you have to. "I don't feel good about how this discussion is going. I think we need a break. Let's just pause to catch our breath and regroup."

This is the power of one. Any one team member has the right to make this request. If you're the one, suggest something like five to ten minutes and check for agreement. If you have the luxury of more time, you might even suggest that people sleep on it before returning to the discussion.

Let everyone step away in the manner that works for them. People may focus on breathing or count to ten, walk outside, stretch, grab a snack, or make a beeline to the teammate who can talk them through calming down. The goal is to settle the intensity of the feelings so your team can listen, speak respectfully, hear each other out, and discuss criticism constructively. The goal is to invite the rational side of people's minds back into the room. A break as brief as five minutes can help people ease their forceful reactions toward moderate levels of emotion.

Emotionally charged moments do arise, even on high-performing teams. They are not necessarily a bad thing. Strong emotions that are suppressed don't just disappear, and charged moments show that your team is engaged deeply. By being prepared to request a break when these moments happen, your team will be better equipped to keep them from becoming a team crisis that derails relationships and your work.

7 Go Ahead and Vent, Briefly and with Purpose

Picture this: it's a sunny day, and you're outside walking barefoot on soft, fresh grass without a care in the world. In all your bliss, you don't notice a sharp piece of wood, and you step on it. This piercing disruption breaks skin and leaves a splinter. Not a life-threatening moment, but certainly uncomfortable and annoying. It's sore, it throbs, and you wonder if it'll get infected. Until it's removed, this distraction is all you can think about. Thankfully, the solution is easy. You don't have to be a surgeon to remove your splinter, and the necessary tools are easy to find. A sanitized tweezer, a steady hand, soap, and water should be all you need to remove it, clean it, and get on with your day.

Teamwork has equally uncomfortable and emotional distractions that happen when we're happily going about our business. Whether they are organizational changes, personal pet peeves among team members, or something else, they certainly won't resolve themselves until we take action. For a big or small splinter, a relatively easy way to remove it is a healthy but brief venting session. Venting as a team releases that throbbing pressure of whatever splinter is compromising your team's ability to focus. Get it out so you can refocus.

Go ahead and vent but do so quickly and with purpose. The first half of a good venting session should be to express honest feelings that are preoccupying you, triggering you, or making you feel like you're not at the top of your game. These feelings contribute to the overall pain of the splinter and will fester if they don't come out. Venting at your team meeting is rarely a scheduled agenda topic, so when the need arises, someone on the team should call it out for what it is. Everyone can be invited to share how they really feel and clear their heads. Speak respectfully and truthfully. This will help release emotion-fueled annoyance and move you toward the second step, a closer look at your annoyance to understand it better. This goal may not be achieved in one session, but once venting begins, your team must complete both steps. Otherwise, your venting will drag people down without leading your team toward progress or purpose. Your ultimate goal is a calmer path forward together.

For a purposeful venting session, share things like:

1. What got us here? What is my take on this situation?

2. How does this make me feel?

3. How do these feelings impact our team and our work?

Then move on to your path forward:

1. What's the real issue at hand? (Not feeling heard. Reacting to changes. Ripple effects on the work.)

2. What's our next step? (Seek outside perspective. Take steps to understand one another better. Communicate more clearly outside the team.)

Don't judge yourselves for the fact that you have splinters—that's totally normal. How deftly you remove your splinters, though, is a differentiator between a stuck team preoccupied with pain and an agile team that can work it out and move on. Using venting sessions purposefully will acknowledge and release distracting emotions and reinforce that there is a time and a way to go about it.

8 Seek Outside Perspective

"While the design is professional and pleasing, the content is full of company jargon, focuses exclusively on your company and your products, and there is almost nothing that demonstrates your interest and understanding of the customer and the challenges they are facing," the consultant explained.

Well, that was eye-opening and a little jarring. Indah, one of the marketing managers, was digesting the consultancy's presentation to her team. As a small marketing and sales team, they had engaged the consultant to review the effectiveness of their customer proposals. They had been proud of how their branded proposal described their company, its history, and its portfolio of great products and services. The outside 'audit' came after losing a bid. It provided an unexpected perspective and objective insights that served as a wake-up call to the team and how their proposal actually looked to clients—thin and jargony.

Like this marketing and sales team did, teams can easily get emotionally stuck and go round and round on issues that team members remain strongly opinionated about. Think about the team that's stuck in frustration, split harshly on what next step to take after their company is acquired, or the team too timid to take a first step as they venture to try an idea no one at their organization has tried before. From the outside looking in, your team's situation is often much clearer to someone else. One of the easiest ways to get unstuck, or test whether your group is on the right track, is to seek outside perspective. Get out of that foggy, angry, or anxious rut by inviting someone who can give your team access to emerging information and unique ideas. Their objective insights may help you clear the air, clear your vision, recognize that your emotions are getting in the way, or prepare your group for next steps.

When it comes to finding the right external perspective, don't ask just anyone. Make sure they have something to contribute to your team's work. Consultants offer knowledge of best practices and a broader scope of what the wider world is doing. Respected peers share interesting views from where they sit. Customer advisory councils and product user groups help keep you close to the customer experience. Team leaders from other departments or top execs can offer missing pieces to your informal communication channels. Even learning how other departments run their meetings, track milestones, or handle stress can be highly enlightening. So, let them hand you their perspective on a platter and see how much it helps your team move past emotional blockages.

Remember, the perspective itself may sting initially. It may take some time and discussion for it to move from hurtful to helpful. The marketing and sales team initially felt defensive under the meticulous gaze of the consultancy, but they quickly came to appreciate their insights—most of which they would not have uncovered on their own. When they chatted later, they had to laugh as they counted the jargon in each proposal and how many pages it took before the customer needs were mentioned! It took this external perspective to help them realize how stuck and internally focused they were.

Help your team gather objective insights in a healthy way by requesting an external perspective. Then, be sure to debrief after the fact. Like Indah's team, restored harmony or break-through innovation are more likely to come after you've had a wake-up call and can see yourselves or your work through that new, external lens.

9 Set Aside Time for Problem-Solving

Haste makes waste! Timing is everything! We have heard these adages and witnessed the mayhem that ensues when they are ignored. Literature and television remind us regularly of the wisdom of well-timed problem-solving. If Romeo and Juliet had avoided hasty decisions, they might have lived. If Marty and Wendy Byrde of the drama series *Ozark* had thought longer before entering the world of a drug kingpin, their lives would be much saner and safer. We read or watch these narratives and find ourselves thinking, Stop! Don't do it! Just think it through!

Why is it, then, that teams often fail to recognize their moments of haste or unwillingness to "think it through?" The answer is that we get caught up in the urgency around us and let our emotions take over.

Here's how a team of financial analysts learned to set aside time for problem-solving to avoid reactive, counter-productive decisions. As a group, they exhibit a high degree of emotion awareness. They share their individual tendencies openly with each other. They know, for instance, that on Friday afternoons, Aman is already looking forward to getting to the lake, and due to his feeling anticipation, he will agree to anything to shorten a meeting. Julia admits that her energy level and ability to listen drop around 3:00 p.m. each day, and she is located on the east coast, so heaven help her west coast teammates after lunch. And Robert gets distressed every time someone mentions upcoming changes. Nevertheless, they accept each other and feel very bonded.

Their chemistry is mostly a good thing, but it's creating one problem. Tangential venting about a myriad of life or work problems pops up in meetings. As they constantly risk running over time and derailing their important discussions, they end up suggesting quick solutions to keep things moving. The problem is that these in-the-moment Band-Aids can't set a broken bone. The team needs to sit down and do some real problem-solving.

Considering their team members' time zones and habits, they agree to implement Think Tank Thursdays at 10:00 am PST, the second Thursday of each month. This meeting is earmarked specifically for problem-solving. Concerns that have surfaced the previous three weeks—whether internal process or collaboration glitches with external teams—are collected in a tracking sheet as they are raised. Then they are discussed at the monthly meeting with the objective of arriving at quality, well-thought-out solutions. Team members receive advance notice about topics, so they arrive having already managed their own feelings around the concerns and are geared up to present possible solutions. The willingness to brainstorm was always present in this group, but no structure existed to support effective problem-solving, at least not prior to Think Tank Thursdays.

Your team's time for problem-solving might not look exactly like Think Tank Thursday, but the strategy is the same. Build on your knowledge of your team's rhythms to carve out the time that works for you and make it happen. The key is creating a mutually agreed-upon structure and designated time that will foster sound thinking and yield quality solutions.

10 Make Better Use of Team Time

Time flies when you're having fun, and it crawls when you feel bored. Both time-bending experiences are backed by science and suggest that time is a curious force to be reckoned with in your team's work. To make the most of your time, first tune in to everyone's feelings. Then, adjust your use of time accordingly.

Team meetings offer one great place to tune in. Once "repeat indefinitely" gets dropped in your team's schedule, the routine creates feelings of boredom as people go on autopilot. Reengage your weary team members with refreshing changes that fit the work. Try reducing how often you meet for a while, and give yourselves the gift of time. Or, if you have a meaty topic underway that will irritate everyone not to finish, stop mid-course and move the topic to a devoted second session. You may also find that changing the length of your meeting can make a big difference. Your thirty-minute weekly check-in could be more efficient and energetic in twenty minutes, or the fifteen-minute logistic-based update is better longer to allow people to share and troubleshoot their challenges. As you see team members' energy waxing or waning, pay attention to what those feelings are telling the team, and adjust your approach.

Another team arena to tune into feelings and time is on an individual level. How do your team members use their time across the work week? Each person may not have complete control over how they make room for thinking time, time to get things done, meeting time, or bonding time, but they will have definite preferences that fit their personal rhythms. As a group, discuss ways to maximize when and where you fit in these very different types of work. What are the days and times of day that help you capitalize on how you feel (e.g., most able to concentrate and focus)? By discussing how to make better use of your time openly and formally, the whole team will learn each other's specific individual preferences. These insights will help everyone respect and optimize important rhythms that propel the work that they do.

Add one last way to protect each other's time: Make it okay or even a team norm to say, "Now is not a good time. How about later?" With open-door policies, people often feel like they can't turn someone away without being rude. The problem with this is that one person's break time can be another's crucial time that week to concentrate.

Time and emotions go hand-in-hand, so tune in to how you're feeling to notice how you're using your time and your teammates' time. Likewise, make better use of your team time to help manage how you're feeling.

11 When Emotions Run High, Rethink Your Team's Approach

As sculptors work on a new piece, they inevitably make mistakes. Usually, they can correct blunders along the way with a bit of finessing, but sometimes the problems are too many or too big to work out. Then, they have to go "back to the chopping block" with a new piece of wood. The same goes for the emotions of a team. When emotions start to run high, your team should treat them like a sculptor treats a mistake. If you can't work through the emotion in real time, that's your group's sign that you need to go back to the chopping block and rethink your approach.

Rethinking your approach is easier said than done. Our brains naturally resist starting from scratch on something we've put time and energy into. On top of that, research shows that extreme emotions get in the way of rational thought. When emotions run high, they can stampede like raging bulls right over your group's ability to think rationally. This, of course, makes it even more difficult for your team to pause and start over. Picture all the poor decisions made by heated, frazzled, worried, bored, or carried away teams.

The key to steering clear of the full impact of destructive feelings is to have a plan in place. That way, when strong feelings arrive, you don't have to get your team to figure out a solution in real time. Instead, you fall back on your plan. Your plan should look something like this: Emotions escalate and begin to take over the group, but someone notices. They bring it to the attention of the group and remind everyone of the goal at hand. Then, as a group, you work backward from the goal to imagine a new way forward—one that isn't so heated. It's a simple plan, but it works wonders to disrupt negative momentum and reinstate a more collaborative frame of mind.

Here's an example. Picture a software sales team at the notoriously boring weekly meeting. People's eyes glaze over, and they only contribute when called on. The VP kicks off the next meeting as bluntly as possible. She says, "I've noticed our meetings are falling flat. I feel like I'm up here delivering a monologue, but I thought the goal of these meetings was to get into discussions about strategy and learn from each other. Let's just start from scratch together. How can we make these meetings more engaging?"

As a team, they begin to work backward from what they want out of the meeting. They decide two people will be responsible for sharing a sales story from the previous month. The story can cover a won or lost sale, strategies used, strategies they wished they used, and what they learned. The meetings almost immediately become an ongoing, dynamic conversation where people learn from each other and add to their sales toolbelts. The meetings are now engaging and certainly more productive. What started as a bad feeling (boredom) smothering the group's productivity ended in resolution for both the boredom and their original goal (practical, strategic meetings).

Emotions and goals are more entwined than you might expect. For that reason, rethinking your approach may come with a pleasant surprise: a clever idea that you might otherwise never pursue.

12 Follow Through on Team Commitments

In April of 2020, a small library in Kentucky known by historians for its local primary resources shut its doors to visitors in response to the pandemic. In their quiet isolation, they committed to making as many of their original materials available electronically as soon as possible. They carefully began to scan and upload documents to their website. For nearly five months, the full team painstakingly gave hours every day to finish. They eventually accomplished what they had set out to do, and the win triggered momentum through an otherwise difficult time. Riding this momentum, they made their next goal to set up a system of organization for all the uploads. Once they'd accomplished that, they set out to improve the website and link it to their social media accounts. In one year, they had changed the very nature of accessibility to their library and were receiving interest from more historians than ever before.

Failing to follow through on your commitments to your team drums up bad feelings as you break expectations. Teammates can feel impatient, worried, preoccupied, or critical of you and others who don't deliver on agreements. After waiting on you to do your part, your teammates begin to feel skeptical about the value of doing their part. Expectations and commitment to the team and the team's work turn to feeling let down, disappointed, alone, resentful, or unmotivated. Those aren't feelings you want seeping into your team relationships. Just as you might feel awful for not living up to a promise, an entire team can feel awful when it doesn't perform reliably.

On the other hand, following through on your commitments can drum up waves of good feelings and momentum. When teammates receive news that your step was taken, they see progress and will feel more cooperative, excited, appreciative, confident, or optimistic for what's to come. Even fulfilling small commitments can evoke many of these feelings and build a sense of group accountability for doing what everyone can to reach future goals. Like the team of librarians accomplishing the arduous transfer of primary source documents to their website, a small yet complete step forward can cause a cascade of positive feelings and results.

Keep in mind though, that it's possible to rev up into a state of zealous excitement where you feel like your team can do anything. At these times, you may find yourselves overcommitting to goals that require more time and energy than you might expect. As a result, those impulsive positive emotions will eventually lose their steam and become less inspiring. When they do, reality sets in and your commitments soon morph into additional pressure, stress, and disappointment.

Push each other through these less inspiring moments

however you can. To drive follow-through, some teams use shared checklists and rigid deadlines for every member, others send someone to check in with people, and others schedule celebrations at checkpoints. There's no best way to do it. Rather, notice what motivates your team and lean on what works for making good on your commitments. Opportunities to build trust and a sense of accomplishment emerge as you plow toward deadlines together.

Emotion Management Strategies

13 Strive to Make the Most of a Bad Situation

Sometimes easy or perfect is not possible. Lingering tough circumstances can cause major aggravations that strain relationships right when your team needs to cooperate most. An emotionally intelligent person can make the most of bad situations, in part, by tolerating frustration and framing their internal thoughts in a positive way. They reassure themselves that they can get through it, they are capable, and that their previous successes will help them now. When your team is faced with bad situations, you can pull together to shape your collective mindset in a positive way as early as possible.

The goal is to be both realistic and positive. Being realistic means avoiding naivete and not blinding yourselves to the situation. A realistic team may also ease their highest standards in the short run if flexing the quality or quantity of team output is possible and not too harmful. Pretending a problem is not there, or not a big deal, will not solve your problem. Doing so even invites difficulties to escalate. Being positive means asserting that your team can handle the repercussions of your situation, has capabilities that will get you through, and is ready to forge ahead. Taking a realistic and positive stance means equal parts accountability, pride, and gratitude. You hold each other accountable for tackling the circumstance as best you can, you take pride in all that your team has achieved in the past, and you make sure to express gratitude that you're in this together.

Think of the team whose lead on their priority project, Ava, takes a job elsewhere. They scramble to cover her responsibilities, but there's no way they can immediately handle them as effectively as she did. The team doesn't have enough time. They're stressed out and irritated with the extra work and the impending need to onboard someone new. For this team, being realistic and positive might look like this: They discuss as a team that they will learn a lot as they cover Ava's role. They don't have to excel in the short run; just get the job done. They give themselves permission to notice opportunities for task improvements as they live in her shoes. They agree any team member can raise the white flag when they feel like they are sinking and state that this bad situation is their chance to prove that no single person can dictate their success as a team.

Your team should draw a firm line in the sand between two key ideas. On the one hand, you can't erase or stifle the way a bad situation makes your team feel. On the other hand, you can't allow your team's reactions to the bad situation to get the best of you. Feeling overwhelmed, shocked, crushed, or paralyzed can quickly spread among the group and block your ability to respond and move forward. Realism and positivity can help prevent this from happening.

It's likely that as your team begins to strive, no one will feel quite ready or on top of it all. Like stretching your muscles after an injury, the first move is difficult and requires you to stretch through aches and stiffness. Your team will be tolerating feelings like worry and insecurity. And like stretching, striving to do your best under tough circumstances is a strained effort that feels both tiring and emotional. It's tiring, but it's worth it. Looking back later, this will be a time your team grew the most. Your team will have newfound strength and resilience. You all persevered through a tough time together and can draw on this experience as you face future bad situations.

14 Give Grief Its Time and Space

No one is prepared for the physical and emotional trauma that grief brings when it enters your team's workspace. Where you work (in offices, open workspaces, classrooms, at home, on a stage, in the field) influences how you interact. Grief traditions that are important to team members, the team culture, and people's personal needs all mix together for a uniquely confusing, difficult period at work. Suddenly and for a while, your team norms don't feel relevant or helpful for knowing what to do or say. Whether your team is grieving the loss of a team member or supporting a team member who is grieving, give grief its time, attention, and space for coping efforts that best fit your group.

The physical trauma of grieving is triggered by the break in the bond with the person lost, all the affection, care, and respect built into the relationship lost (the emotional trauma of grieving). Knowing about the physical symptoms of this break may help you spot them and decide whether to take steps to soothe them or give time and space for them to pass. The physical pain of grief is caused by an overwhelming amount of stress hormones released throughout the grieving process in response to your loss. These hormones effectively stun the muscles they contact. Symptoms like chest pain or pressure, shortness of breath, faintness, anxiety, back pain, stiffness, headaches, queasy stomach, loss of appetite, binge eating, irritable bowel syndrome, insomnia, and exhaustion are all common but typically ease over 6 months.

There are no rule books, deadlines, or sequential steps for grieving teams, but there is practical advice from a 2017 study in the American Journal of Hospice and Palliative Medicine. Here are six guideposts for you and your team during the months after a significant loss. Lean on them as you, your team, or a teammate keeps going even through feeling numb, distracted, fatigued, or profoundly sad.

1. **Food Guidepost.** Stress triggers cravings for sugar and fat, and mourning traditions may compel you to bring in feel-good, high-calorie and high-fat processed food for the team. Yet these foods can make you feel worse. Try to keep up a well-balanced diet. That means eating plenty of vegetables, fruits, and lean proteins and drinking plenty of water.

2. **Sleep Guidepost.** Grieving expends intense energy and can disrupt sleep (trouble falling asleep, waking up often, or trouble waking up). For the best shot at restful sleep, try to keep a regular bedtime and sleep routine and avoid caffeine or alcohol in the evening.

3. **Exercise Guidepost.** Temporarily set aside more strenuous fitness goals when sorrow is sapping your motivation and energy. Instead, teammates can go for a lunchtime walk or seek a walk with a friend after work, as moving can help ease depression and distraction from anxiety.

4. **Teamwork Guidepost.** The loss of a teammate may require taking over certain job responsibilities in the short run. Unexpected difficulty concentrating and errors can create additional stress. Be compassionate with yourself and each other, and try to reframe thoughts of feeling overwhelmed with this encouraging reminder. Tasks help keep your mind focused, distracted from your grief for a short while, and move you closer to the bond that you had with your teammate as you honor the work that they did.

5. **Self-Care Guidepost.** Prioritize caring for your health by getting meticulous about your vitamins, medications, and health appointments. Ask a teammate or friend to help schedule or remind you of upcoming appointments and prescription refills, and set reminders in multiple places (computer, phone, watch, or Post-its on your monitor) so you don't miss them.

6. **Social Care Guidepost.** The team is perfectly seated to provide social care and support to each other. If teammates

are receptive, do indulge yourselves. Daily connections with your teammates remind you that you are not alone. Weekly get-togethers for lunch or coffee or a monthly potluck (even if virtual) are all wonderful ways to share memories or just listen to how things are going for each other.

Grief takes intense energy. For a while, your team might consider your work and your relationships as less important or engaging. Temporary withdrawal from each other, expressing feelings of loss, supporting one another, and eventually reinvesting in the team and its work all help heal your grief. How you cope and support each other is a memorable experience. Pay attention to how people grieve uniquely and be open and flexible to the differences. Do your best to support each person the way they want to be supported, and don't pass up opportunities to show that you care, even when a reciprocal response may not come your way.

7

—

INTERNAL RELATIONSHIP STRATEGIES

Have you ever been part of a team where people can almost read each other's minds? It can feel like this. A group is problem-solving for a while when suddenly someone says, "No, wait. Are you thinking what I'm thinking?" Another says, "Oh yeah. This is exactly like when Gary did that thing that worked that one time. Right?" After hands cover mouths, giggling "no way!" and looking around at each other waiting to burst, a third says, "You're right! With a little adjustment, we could be close. I think this will help us nail it!" Then assignments and offers to dig in fill the room.

If you were there observing, you'd be clueless as to what they were talking about but marveling at how they interact and how tightly they communicate. Their bonds, fun, history, and ability to read each other aren't just things that happen overnight. It takes time and investment in the team's relationships as well as mutual experiences dealing with a myriad of situations.

To build or strengthen your team's relationships, you will have parallel work to the work handed to you by your employer. A thoughtful approach is to choose one actionable relationship strategy to work on together for now. Working too hard or spending an inordinate amount of time on relationships can feel overwhelming or distract you from your work. That makes your efforts feel forced or intrusive. Relationships are a collection of many little interactions, so the nature and quality of interactions are the material you will be molding and shaping over time.

The 14 strategies in this chapter will remind you of both natural ways and crafted-by-the-team ways to form healthy relationships. If you've ever needed reasons to allow fun and positivity to enter your workspace, some of these strategies are your permission slips. You'll soon see that laughing and talking during retreats and fun getaways are like taking vitamins to strengthen your immune system. You'll learn how to look back on your team's memories and history in service to the future and how to deal with moments in the present that get in your team's way. Most importantly, you'll have actionable strategies for handling the universal difficulties that undermine relationships inside a team.

INTERNAL RELATIONSHIP STRATEGIES

1. Encourage Team Bonding
2. Have Fun and Laugh
3. Value the Small Things
4. Meet Offsite
5. Use Words of Support and Help Each Other
6. Communicate Clearly with One Another
7. Respect One Another's Differences
8. Focus on What the Group Can Control
9. Tap Into History, to a Degree
10. Challenge Ideas Constructively
11. Remember the Wins
12. Be Open to Feedback from Each Other
13. Have that Tough Conversation Directly
14. Work Through a Conflict

Internal
Relationship
Strategies

1 Encourage Team Bonding

Elaborate campuses with slides, bars, and yoga studios are great to have, but research shows that, more than anything, your team needs time together to bond.

To help the lowest-performing teams at a call center, researchers asked their manager to try something simple: take a coffee break together at the same time every day. The manager was not thrilled at the idea of leaving their phones unattended for fifteen minutes, but desperate to improve his teams' performance, he agreed to try it. In only weeks, the average handling time (the gold-standard metric in call centers) improved 20% on the lowest-performing teams, and employee satisfaction leaped 10%. What had changed? Communication between members was more energetic and more engaged.

This example shows how there's no right or wrong way to encourage team bonding. It's a strategy you can employ right away and for free. Choose something that feels natural to your group, and then carve out a plan. You could imitate the call center team and meet together daily for a fifteen-minute break. You can play online trivia on a video call. You could have monthly lunches where a few team members grab lunch together or go for a walk. One team we know did monthly happy hours with one rule: You absolutely could not talk about work. If you did, you had to contribute five dollars toward next month's happy hour.

Most people spend about half their waking day with their team. Getting to know the people around you isn't just about improving performance or engagement. It's ultimately about having fun and developing meaningful relationships in that half of your life.

2 Have Fun and Laugh

You are running late for the 8:00 am team meeting and feeling unprepared as you race into the conference room, trying not to trip over anyone's chair. Everyone is engrossed in their phones taking care of last-minute messages, but they still notice your rushed entrance and slightly disheveled appearance. You grab an available seat, catch your breath, and glance down at your feet. Your eyes widen at what you see, and the pit in your stomach is even heavier.

"Are you good, Gabe?" Your mind freezes for a moment on this thought. How much worse are you about to make this?

"Well, it's been a bit of a tough morning. I got dressed in the dark so I wouldn't wake my wife after her night shift, didn't have time for coffee, and now I need to confess." You look down at your feet again. "I've just realized that I'm wearing two different shoes—a black and a brown loafer."

The room breaks into laughter. You can't help but smile and laugh as well. Teammates look under the table to see for themselves. They laugh, and two people share stories of their own embarrassing but laughable moments while one team member heads to the coffee machine to make sure you get some caffeine in your system before you make any mistakes that matter.

The mood in the room has changed 180 degrees. Smiles and laughter have taken over, and your vulnerable moment draws everyone closer.

It's exactly the nourishment your team needed, and it took up little time and no planning. The lighter tone impacts the rest of the meeting as team members cheerfully share their project updates. There is a feeling of renewed energy and readiness to then focus on achieving the team's quarterly goals. In that moment, you recalled the advice of one of your mentors: "Take your work seriously, but don't take yourself too seriously."

Research studies prove that not only is laughter catchy, but it impacts happiness and productivity. Smiling and laughter reduce stress through the release of dopamine, endorphins, and serotonin and put you in a better mood. Importantly, happiness at work leads to increased performance, and greater happiness in your home life, too. Creating an environment where there is positivity, fun, and high energy will nourish the whole team.

Having fun and laughing together can surface at any moment. The trick is knowing that it is a two-step strategy and one that you can't force. Doing so will kill its spontaneity. Step one, spark positivity. Step two, delight in the fun. Find your group's unique chemistry for igniting positivity. Meeting offsite (Strategy #4) can help your group find chemistry outside of work, but then be sure to bring that positivity back on the job together. When positive energy materializes, don't

Internal
Relationship
Strategies

be afraid to revel in it for a few minutes. Don't ignore it, cut it off, or squash it.

The research-backed benefits of laughter give you permission to stop any negative thoughts or feelings about fun at work. A team that takes their work seriously but doesn't take themselves too seriously will be a higher-performing, happier team—even when wearing mismatched shoes.

3 **Value the Small Things**

Acorns® is an investing app with a very simple yet effective idea. Whenever you make a purchase by credit or debit card, the app rounds up to the nearest dollar, taking what would be the "spare change" from your transaction and investing it for you. The tiny transactions add up over time, and people find that their hundreds of transactions equate to hundreds of dollars they wouldn't have otherwise invested. Their investments, of course, then grow over the years. Twenty years down the line, these little acorns suddenly add up to something much bigger and more impactful. For teams, small positive gestures are like social acorns of kindness and fun. They can add up over time to make a world of difference. That's why highly functioning teams care as much about fitting in the small things as they do about working on the big stuff to achieve their lofty goals.

Sure, it is difficult to focus on or even remember small things when challenging deadlines compel you to push aside everything else. Just don't push aside seemingly insignificant things that are extremely beneficial to your team's life force—things like saying "thank you" or "I'm sorry" to each other, greeting people by name, acknowledging a team member's bad day, offering to help each other, or following up on how a team member is doing. Further examples include things like sharing inside jokes or a fond memory, celebrating progress, texting a grateful emoji, remembering a birthday, milestone, or showing appreciation for people's extra efforts. Your team can try to double or triple this list with creative ways to value the small things that fit your team's style of working together.

4 **Meet Offsite**

Axe throwing, bonding with wild horses, a ropes course, a yacht excursion, that hotel conference center with a spa, or gathering in the park under a canopy followed by a barbeque and volleyball. They all work because they strengthen the relationships among team members and build team morale, allowing the opportunity for everyone to get to know each other better. In a relaxed way, people can learn about each other's perspectives, work styles, and strengths without the usual stress or distractions of day-to-day work. You can even use an offsite to tackle a high-profile priority together.

Here's how to put together your offsite. Start getting people excited and collaborating ahead of time by asking everyone to weigh in on the activity and vote for their favorite. Or surprise them. Next, create a structure to keep things on track, one that works well for your team, your activity, and your objectives. Don't replicate the weekly agenda the team has on its plate at the time—that's what offices and virtual meetings are for. If you want to accomplish a tangible set of decisions, you'll want to use a more structured approach that breaks down topics, discussions, timeframes, and target outcomes. If your goal is interpersonal, just getting to know each other better, you might structure just a couple essential topics and devote more time to team building, bonding, or even just conversation over dinner. The idea is usually to look up and out at your team's future or look inward and pause in a more relaxed, creative environment.

Don't forget the coda to a productive offsite. The following week, check in at your team meeting about what insights or next steps you want to build into working together. Even after a socially oriented offsite, this is a great way to have team members reflect on what they learned about each other, look back at a few fun or funny pictures, and commit to doing this again sometime. Think of the entire offsite process as three phases—plan before, relax and bond during, reflect after.

Activities outside the office strengthen your team's relationship skills. They create a common positive experience, spark new traditions, build memories together, establish a common vocabulary, and spawn running jokes. Offsite meetings just might be the difference between a team that gets along well and an extremely close team with that "something special" you can't quite put your finger on.

5 Use Words of Support and Help Each Other

What's the right thing to say when times are tough? That depends. When's the best time to say it? That also depends. Who should share these words of support? You get the picture. It depends.

Why does it depend? Because your team is like a fingerprint. It's one-of-a-kind and unlike any other team you've been a member of. That's why there is no one-size-fits-all recipe for what to say, when to say it, or who should say it. If your team leader says, "We can do this!" in a cheery, confident tone immediately after getting some discouraging news, it may come across as out-of-touch and inappropriately sugary. But if you follow that with a more sincere tone and say, "We've done this before, I know we're capable of doing it again," you can strike that right balance of motivation and sensitivity.

Your team is unique, so how you approach your words of support must fit your group. Your emotion awareness skills will cue you in to the feelings or moods that are present. Then find the best support for your team in that moment. If you know your team well, you know which words of support fall flat, which words help them rise up, and when these words are needed. However, it's remembering to say them out loud that counts.

Though your team is unique, keep in mind that words of support do share some universal qualities. First, the words should remind everyone of your team's belief in what you can do. Reminding people of a past success can help make this resonate better and feel more authentic. Second, the words should address how people are feeling. If, for example, your team momentarily lacks confidence, use words that will reassure them. Third, the person delivering the message should be credible for the situation and believe what they are saying. This could be the most tenured team member with history, the newest team member who has a fresh, spot-on perspective, or anyone in between. Carefully chosen words of support should recenter, refocus, and rally everyone together as a unit. You may even surprise yourself and find that your words reassure yourself too.

6 Communicate Clearly with One Another

"I wish Donna communicated as well over email and by phone as she does in person. Reading her messages is like deciphering a secret code, and she sounds so blunt over the phone!" Teammates make comments about poor communication on emotional intelligence assessments all the time. The unfortunate thing is that these miscommunications are as costly as they are common. Teams waste countless hours desperately second-guessing what was really meant. Worse yet, miscommunications can exasperate people, sap their energy, and drive a wedge in their team's relationships.

One of the things that makes clear communication so difficult is that people rarely prefer to send and receive information in the same way. That's why something as seemingly simple as a "reply all" email can be so contentious. To some people, a reply all email is overwhelming, and they don't want to be included unless it's directly relevant and actionable. Others feel excluded and undervalued if they are not looped in on the news or the fun. Neither view is right or wrong. It's just a matter of preference.

Add more substantial preferences than reply all, like those stemming from personality traits and learning styles, and you can quickly see how complex it is to communicate clearly. Personality differences stem from tendencies like how energetic, agreeable, open to experiences, organized, and sensitive each of your teammates is. These traits vary in unique ways for each person. It requires you, as their teammate, to begin noticing their preferences for receiving messages, news, bad news, and the like. Learning styles also influence the ways that people on your team take in and retain ideas and messages. Visual learners want to see it. Auditory learners want to hear it or talk about it. Kinesthetic learners want to do it, and learners who need to think on it do best when they have time to reflect on it.

Begin to better communicate with each teammate by noticing how they each like to communicate with you. Pay attention to how they send messages and ask them how they prefer to receive them. A note on a chair may be appreciated or resented, and gratitude may be best shared publicly or privately. You should discover preferences or pet peeves like these asap. When absolute clarity is critical or urgent, you must communicate using the methods that will have the best chance of success.

As a team, you can discuss methods that will support clear communication. Who should be copied on correspondence related to certain topics? Are cameras always on during video conferencing? On conference calls, how will you clarify who is speaking and avoid talking over each other? Whether in-person or virtual, will meetings have agendas and timekeepers? What is the expected response time to written messages? Address these communication challenges now to save frustration and confusion later.

No matter how prepared you are, miscommunication will happen. Consider adding one more effort that involves the whole team. Everyone on the team can agree to speak up when a message is confusing or doesn't come across the way they think it was intended. This timely feedback will help the whole team clear up unclear communication on the fly.

7 Respect One Another's Differences

Four team members in a 4 x 100-meter relay sprint at different speeds, but it's the team's collective running time that determines the outcome of the race. For the fastest combined pace, the second-fastest runner begins, followed by the third-fastest, then the slowest, and finally the anchor, who is the fastest runner. Rather than impede the team's ability to perform, the team's internal differences are recognized, appreciated, and employed strategically to compete and (hopefully) win the race. Each runner plays a unique and consequential role in the team's overall performance.

There are a great many things that make up the differences among team members, both surface-level differences people can see (like body language, facial expressions, demeanor, etc.) and deep-level differences (like emotions, traits, attitudes). So, what does team EQ add to the story? Research shows that deep differences threaten group cohesion, and team EQ skills can remove that threat. That's because relationship skills enable your team to nurture deep-level diversity as a resource for team performance. Tapping into your deep differences as resources instead of obstacles fosters respect— feeling seen, heard, understood, and appreciated. Respect allows differing viewpoints to flourish in an environment of support, admiration, and collaboration. Your team's deep level differences help you see new angles in multi-dimensional problems, explore new directions, or strategize effective ways of working together.

Respecting one another's differences means inviting them in and the benefits they bring to the team. Perhaps that sounds easier said than done. Let's agree that for conflicts around deep differences, there may be a need to combine team EQ strategies (see Strategy 38 for conflicts). But prior to conflicts, respecting one another's differences is about allowing them into the room. Imagine how different you would feel to hear teammates say, "Where did you get that idea?" versus, "I never thought of it like that before." The first reply is critical and suggests, "you are over there, and we are over here." The second is welcoming and implies a new door may be opening for consideration. Other statements that embrace differences are:

- "I always enjoy hearing how you look at things."

- "Your take on that is so new for me and so cool."

- "I want to think about what you've said and how you feel about it."

Differences can be your team's greatest resource or a relentless barrier. The decisive factor is how your team will manage their potential. Find your differences, share them, and respect them. That's the beginning. Once your team enjoys each other's differences and is used to having divergent approaches in play, then you can begin using them strategically.

8 Focus on What the Group Can Control

We've all been there at some point: So caught up in a sudden obstacle and the stress that goes with it that we freeze up like a deer in headlights. Imagine the chaos on the day before the game when the 2020 Denver Broncos football team were told that all four of their quarterbacks couldn't play—they'd either tested positive for Covid-19 or been deemed a "close contact." Athletes at the highest level rely on their pre-game routines, and it's hard to imagine that the news didn't throw their mental preparation off track in a significant way.

When your team faces unexpected difficulties, your emotions can easily take over your ability to perform. Caught up in things outside your control, it becomes more difficult to give 100% of your attention, easier to overlook key details, and more likely that you'll miss a deadline. That's why it's especially important in times of high stress and intense emotion to refocus on what your group can control.

A seasoned Broncos player can step up during the shocking outbursts the day before the game to say, "Hey guys, cool it for a sec. This decision was out of our hands, and it feels like an outrageous situation, but we're here to play." This simple acknowledgment that the effects of external forces are outside your team's control serves as a grounding reality check.

Ask yourselves what your responsibility is to the bigger picture. Do you have tasks or deadlines to meet that will affect the overall project? In the case of the Broncos, it was each player's responsibility to make sure his head was still in the game and ready to play his position.

No, they didn't win. The practice squad rookie receiver Kendall Hinton stepped in as quarterback and completed just one of nine passes as the Broncos lost 31-3. Directing their energies toward what was within their control at least enabled them to get out on the field and play.

What you don't want to do is be the team member who derails your team's project or efforts because you've been focused on matters that aren't yours to control. Focus on what is your responsibility and let whoever owns the issue figure it out. You may be needed to step up for the team and be at your best, and that is all you can prepare for.

9 Tap into History, to a Degree

We've all heard that "history always repeats itself." It is the reason why tapping into your team's history can inform your team of your present reality and help you better understand the context of your current situation. That said, history never repeats itself exactly. Take a peek at Mark Twain's view on how the past manifests in the present:

> *History never repeats itself, but the kaleidoscopic combinations of the pictured present often seem to be constructed out of the broken fragments of antique legends.*

This description points to the complicated role your team's history plays. Some team members work to preserve it, and others work to discard it. Neither of these approaches is bad, and each has its time and place. Consider both as you tap into your team's history, to a degree.

There's wisdom to be found in your midst if your team cares to ask your more tenured team members. And those who were around before should offer their perspective when the team doesn't think to ask. Understanding how and why things were done in the past is a way to value interpersonal lessons already learned. It's also an effective way to make sure the same mistakes aren't made again and again. Revisiting your team's history may even help you rediscover lessons learned that are valuable to your team's work today.

The reason not to overdo it when it comes to tapping into your team's history is to make sure your group doesn't get stuck in Mark Twain's "antique legends." If your team's storied past has become larger than life or veiled in mysteries, it may not offer much to learn from now. Discuss the relevance of these stories and the unspoken norms that have carried through to your team today. It may be time to allow the present team's needs and your future priorities to inform new approaches and paths forward.

10 **Challenge Ideas Constructively**

In writing workshops, the entire premise is for writers to challenge each other's work and ideas to help each other learn and grow. Feelings are almost always in a heightened state as writers share work that's near and dear to them. It's not uncommon to see people leave a successful workshop motivated and beaming. It's also not uncommon for writers to leave an unsuccessful workshop crushed or even crying. Sure, part of this intense spectrum of reactions is because of the heightened stakes of sharing something so personal, but more often than not, how someone feels leaving their workshop has to do with the way their ideas and writing were challenged.

The difference lies in whether a critique is destructive or constructive. Destructive feedback makes the recipient feel their idea isn't worthy, they aren't capable, or they should have known better. In other words, it critiques or shames the person as much as the work. Challenging ideas in an unskilled or destructive way divides team members and makes the whole team afraid to discuss any type of criticism more deeply. Constructive criticism, on the other hand, aims to build on ideas shared. Replace these three types of destructive challenges with constructive challenges to team member ideas:

1. **Instead of pointing to problems, offer improvements.** Don't point out all the flaws in someone's idea as a way of saying that the idea won't work. Instead, ask your team, "How might we address ___?" Now you're focused on improving a small piece that isn't yet there. This can help improve the idea and flesh out further dimensions in real time. Better yet, offer a potential fix as you point out the problem. When you do this, you signal respect for the other person's idea and a willingness to collaborate and take their work to the next level. This kind of optimistic support spreads among the team.

2. **Instead of saying "I like" or "I dislike," offer examples and data.** The worst critiques come from a place of ego or personal opinion. No one is expecting you to be judge and jury. Take out the "me vs. you" and turn all eyes toward researched information. When you use examples and data to critique, you offer a more valuable, objective look. You help everyone see the problem you're raising more clearly. Perhaps most importantly, examples make your critique less personal and bring the issue you're thinking about to life.

3. **Instead of replacing another's bad idea with your great one, stack or intersect the two ideas.** While your opposing idea might be valuable, try to think how it might already relate to the existing one or build on the foundation

the first idea laid. It's rare that ideas and solutions are completely independent. Use phrases like, "I think what I'm about to share relates to what you just described," or "Let me add to your idea."

Constructive criticism is a pillar for good relationships among team members. It often is the difference between a relationship-damaging argument and a free-flowing collaboration where the quality of your team's ideas surpasses that of any one individual. Making it a team norm to criticize constructively can not only help make your team's work better (just look at all the novelists thanking their writing groups on the first page of their acknowledgments) but also help build relationships, foster a trusting environment, create an atmosphere of lifelong learning, and inspire and empower innovation.

11   **Remember the Wins**

In your team's drive for excellence, you focus on the things that need attention and repair, and you diminish or ignore the wins you've achieved. There's no time for celebration or even acknowledgment. Does this sound like your team? If you're not careful, this mindset can become a habitual way of thinking, an emotional drag that weighs your team down. When your team is in this space, inspiration may be hard to find on the days when it's needed.

Any one teammate can begin to turn your team's mindset around by purposefully refocusing the group on your past wins. Reflect on a time the team faced a challenge and overcame it. Point out how impossible that challenge felt and how well the group responded. Say things like, "Remember all the terrible things that could have happened, and we side stepped them all!" It might sound obvious, but past feel-good moments still feel good as you relive them. They are the fuel that can power the team forward to more confidently face the present.

To practice this strategy, start a conversation about your team's proudest moments where you faced difficulties and over-came them. Maybe it was a time when the odds were stacked against you, and the chances of a win were unlikely. Somehow, some way, you pulled it off! As you read this, you might already have an example in mind. If you're already smiling or feeling a sense of pride or lightness, keep your example for that day when you can be the one to pull your team up and out of feeling discouraged.

When your team surfaces a few proud moments, it is worth a walk through the specifics of each win to keep the details fresh in your team's memory—like you're back in that moment. What were the circumstances? How did you pull off the win? Answer the "who, what, where, when, why, and how" of your achievement. When you visualize it with this level of detail, you are dusting off the past and making the win real again. It also makes the win easier to remember the next time you need a boost. It's no longer tucked away as a vague, distant memory.

Practicing this strategy will not prevent the challenges that come your way. Instead, it will change how you face them with a collective can-do attitude. Remembering your team's wins prepares you with an arsenal of memories and good feelings that you can quickly queue up to remind your group that you've won before, how you've won before, and that you can win again. You're really beginning to record a big piece of your team's history—something you can draw strength and meaning from for years to come.

12 Be Open to Feedback from Each Other

At the team meeting, after you gave your update, Roland leans over and whispers, "You talk in circles when you're not prepared." *Ouch, Roland!* Now you feel embarrassed. You can't stop thinking about it. *Is it true? Have others noticed this? Why does this hurt? Were you wasting everyone's time? Should you do something about it? Can you even do something about it? Ouch.*

If you could see your brain hooked up to an MRI at the moment feedback hurts your feelings, you'd see the pain centers in your brain light up, the same areas that light up when you skin your knee. That is why feedback literally stings and why so many people aren't open to feedback. Instead, they go into a protective mode to avoid pain rather than a receptive mode to seek growth.

Whether mild or harsh, feedback reveals how your good intentions, skills, moods, habits or mistakes surface into your words and actions with teammates. When you get feedback, especially from a teammate, it means there's a problem getting in your way or getting in your teammates' way. To ignore it means you're likely going to stumble over this problem again, and now you may begin annoying other teammates. That's not growth. That's a bad habit.

So be open to feedback from teammates. It will take some internal encouragement. Remind yourself that it's normal to feel the sting. It's also healthy to take a little time to let the sting subside. Next, try to absorb the feedback by studying it further. The feedback itself may offer a better path forward.

With Roland's feedback, the path forward is to plan ahead for project updates. One option is to spend 15 minutes preparing some bulleted key points. This gives you an extra day to get your questions answered or to prepare a few data points. Now you feel ready. You'll be on point, brief, and clear in your next update. No more talking in circles. Roland's feedback doesn't feel so hurtful now. It was really helpful, and only because you were open to it.

When feedback is positive, be gracious and thank the person who spots your shining moment and cares enough to let you know. When feedback is negative, still be gracious and thank the person who spots your misstep and cares enough to let you know. Then take the time you need to feel it, absorb it, accept it, study it, and decide what the better path forward for you will be.

As a team, you want to encourage openness to feedback. The brief moments of pain or discomfort will be far outweighed by the benefits. You'll create a team culture of authenticity and growth instead of fake kindness or fear.

13 Have that Tough Conversation Directly

Of all the written comments made on team EQ assessments, one of the most common sounds something like this: "I'm so tired of hearing my teammate complain to me about other people on the team. I wish they would just have that conversation directly instead of bringing their negativity my way."

Why is this comment so frequent? The obvious answer is that complaining behind someone's back feels like a quick fix—the easiest way to release pent-up emotions. Complaining offers a kind of temporary relief as you unload your anger, frustration, or disappointment onto someone else.

The problem is that while complaining provides temporary relief for you, complaints don't solve the issue. They also generate deeper complications. You weigh your teammates down as they listen to and absorb your negative feelings. When you complain, your negative opinion can fester and grow, while the person causing your suffering doesn't even know. These thoughts will inevitably continue to bother you as you bypass opportunities to address your teammate about what you are feeling.

The same goes for passive aggression. Angry quips passed off as jokes might help you feel better for a moment, but they set a negative and uncomfortable tone for everyone else on your team. Whatever might be holding you back, remind yourself that you owe it to the other person and to your team to have that tough conversation directly.

To have that tough conversation, you first need to get yourself, your thoughts, and your feelings in order. Your emotions may be holding you back from this conversation—fear, frustration, discomfort, and anxiety. Remind yourself that these kinds of conversations are rarely as bad as you expect them to be, especially if you plan ahead. With care and attention, they can turn into a positive, mutually beneficial conversation, and they most certainly will create relief for the team as peace returns to the atmosphere.

Next, prepare the points you want to make during the conversation. Think about your goal with the conversation and find a mutually beneficial purpose that you can point the conversation toward as you begin.

When you begin the actual conversation, communicate two things as clearly as possible: mutual purpose and mutual respect. Open by sharing with the other person why this conversation is important (mutual purpose) to you, to the work, and, you hope, to them. Thank them for hearing your experience and share that you are interested in hearing theirs.

As the tough part of the conversation follows, describe how your teammate's words and actions impact you and your work.

Watch your words and actions as carefully as possible. Avoid going silent too long, getting combative, or making it personal. If you find your emotions building and starting to interfere with your focus on the conversation, it is perfectly fine to take a breath to refocus. Then, restate your planned purpose. This is your anchor to keep the conversation respectful and meaningful. Listen carefully to their experience, ask questions, give them time to speak and think, and don't be afraid to use moments of silence to reflect or wait for a response.

You will find that more often than not, your festering emotions were just that: festering. By bringing these difficult conversations out of your head and directly over to your teammate sooner rather than later, you can proactively solve the issue while maintaining your relationships with all your teammates. You may even impress them with your courage to try.

There's another important part of this strategy that will inevitably come your way. When you hear one of your teammates complaining about someone, and you don't appreciate the negative impact it has on you, encourage them to have that conversation directly. Offer to help them sort through how to describe the issue without sounding like they are on the offensive. When you and your teammates help each other approach difficult conversations directly, you are investing deeply in your team's relationships.

14 Work Through a Conflict

A 1991 study of the group dynamics within 20 string quartets found that the most successful quartets handled conflict in a special and highly effective way. They understood each other well enough to know what could and couldn't be said. They knew each other's hot buttons and knew how to avoid pushing them during heated discussions. They were careful to hear each other out because they felt minority dissatisfaction caused problems. When the team size is just four, and they each sit close while playing beautiful music in front of an audience, conflict among the group can ruin performance.

There's a lot that any team can learn from their approach to conflict. Task and process conflicts are about the work itself, and relationship conflicts are more about personal issues such as dislike among group members and feelings like annoyance, disappointment, frustration, or irritation. Often, the two intersect, and when the work conflict is addressed, the relationship difficulties soften.

There are steps you can take to focus on the work conflict first that will help you navigate your relationship successfully. Start by mentioning your understanding of where you both agree, even if it's a very small part of the conflict. Mention also that you are interested in working through this together.

Next, ask your teammate to help you understand their thoughts while resisting the urge to plan your rebuttal or express rising negative emotions. Remember, negative emotions are catchy and expressing them will distract you from turning the next half of the conversation over to your teammate. When your teammate is finished, you can share your understanding of what they just shared (Let me see if I heard you correctly.). Request a similar opportunity to share your viewpoint and help them understand where you're coming from. Now talk together about options for resolving the conflict, treating both sides as valid. The final critical step is to decide your next actions together, even if they are as simple as to keep talking or check in on how things are going.

The truth is, if your team makes use of other team EQ strategies, you'll have a full toolbelt at your disposal as you attempt to fix each part of a conflict (the task or process, and the relationship). Surface the quieter feelings, understand one another, respect each other's differences, hear people out, challenge ideas constructively, step back, take a break, strive to make the most of a bad situation, and so on. These strategies will all help you effectively navigate emotional dynamics that kick up before and during team conflicts.

Be careful about shifting your statements about the work into statements about your emotions (You make me so mad!) or their character (You're so hard to work with!). These are signs that your feelings are hijacking your ability to effectively manage yourself in the conflict. Instead, take a breath. Say you're sorry, and you want to rephrase that. Then, attach your feelings only to yourself (It's so hard for me to work well when ___, and I find myself feeling frustrated because I can't ___.). Keep it about the work.

When you attach any element of a conflict to who your teammate is as a person or what they value most, you threaten their very seat on the team. This causes intense mutual bad feelings and can feel as though the only way to resolve the conflict would be for someone to leave the team. Instead, when team members know how to talk about problem behaviors (When you said or did that, this is how it affects me or my work.) and avoid talking about personal qualities (You're so this or that.), the conflict conversation remains focused on helping your team excel.

One study shows just how important it is to handle the emotional side of team conflicts. After observing a team in conflict for just 15 minutes, researchers were able to identify with 91% accuracy which teams were low-performing and which were high-performing. To make this determination, they looked for just two things: the balance between positive and negative emotions and the number of negative actions they considered to be hostile.

8

—

EXTERNAL RELATIONSHIP STRATEGIES

Think back to your first days as a new employee. You were likely greeted by your supervisor and introduced to the people working near you (some of them teammates) and then shown to your workspace. Perhaps over the first couple of weeks, you continued to meet other people, but for the most part, you were welcomed onto a team, and then your work began. Throughout many organizations, this way of onboarding is normal. Teams don't spend much time together looking out and around the organization, so why would they make it a part of your onboarding process? You might think that looking out and around the organization is the team leader's job or the job of the department head, but it's your whole team's job, especially when it comes to building relationships. There's a world of people out there working on your organization's mission, and the sooner your team invests in your relationships with them, the sooner your work will also benefit.

Here is the business case for giving extra time and energy to your team's external relationships. Teams' contributions are measured, in part, by how well they meet the needs of their organization. Teams who work well together but whose relationships don't extend beyond their insular team will often struggle to understand or meet the greater needs of the organization. They work in a sort of vacuum, blissfully unaware of their potential for greater impact, depriving themselves of opportunities to stand out or win important resources and attention. On the other hand, teams that seek out and develop strong external relationships can grow their understanding of the bigger picture more quickly. They can learn from their external relationships and develop a greater context for how they fit into their organization's bigger picture. They can then use this understanding to seek out opportunities for a larger and more strategic impact.

Organizations depend on collaboration between teams. Yet, at the same time, poor cross-functional collaboration is a problem. A common reason organizations bring us onsite to train them in emotional intelligence is to help them overcome issues with cross-functional communication and siloed departments. Growing and managing your team's outside relationships is the best way to bridge the cross-functional gap.

When your team is skilled in your relationships, your group becomes a role model of sorts, positively showcasing and adding team EQ skills to your company culture. Your healthy interactions with outsiders can spark innovative ideas and improve the work atmosphere when visitors, customers, vendors, or prospective candidates enter your office or virtual work rooms.

This chapter provides 14 strategies for building and managing relationships outside your team. They are crafted to help your group invest in the relationships that are interconnected with your team and with your company priorities. Sure, you can downplay the importance of people outside your team, but doing so can create hurdles to achieving quality work, accessing resources, or meeting tight deadlines. Neglecting external relationships can also build walls around your team's visibility and aspirations. Some of these strategies are quick and easy to add to your relationship repertoire, a few give you permission to enjoy the people around you, and others offer new insights you'll have to think hard about. All the strategies in this chapter will help your team make sure you are doing your part to strengthen the external relationships your team relies on to achieve its goals.

External
Relationship
Strategies

EXTERNAL RELATIONSHIP STRATEGIES

1. Understand the Broader Environment
2. Win Confidence with Quality Work
3. Leverage Team Members' Relationship Strengths
4. Communicate Clearly Outside the Team
5. Build Bridges
6. Host Visitors as Guests
7. Deepen Bonds with Other Teams
8. Celebrate Bigger
9. Increase Your Team's Visibility
10. Take Matters into Your Own Hands
11. Avoid Pointing Fingers
12. Own Your Mistakes
13. Frame Requests to the Mission
14. Tackle a Wider Problem

1 **Understand the Broader Environment**

Your cardiovascular system moves blood, nutrients, oxygen, carbon dioxide, and hormones around the body. The critical parts in this system are the heart, blood, arteries, and veins. Everything begins and ends with your heart, which pumps blood out through your arteries and back through your veins. While your heart, blood, and blood vessels perform unique functions, they are interconnected and depend on one another for their own health and the health of the broader system. We can't truly understand what the heart does and ensure it functions properly unless we understand the cardiovascular system in which the heart operates.

The same can be said of your team. How your group operates to perform at your best is interconnected with other teams, and vice versa, in service of a healthy, growing organization. Unlike the human body, teams where you work do not automatically, effortlessly work together. Your team has to intentionally look outward to understand your broader environment and your place within it.

Here's how to get started: First, think about how influence flows in your organization. Learn more about the teams that influence your team and how your team influences them in

External Relationship Strategies

return. Observe how they handle normal situations and how they deal with matters of stress and urgency. Approach teams and key players in your sphere to ask about their goals, works in progress, challenges, needs, and concerns. What is important to them? How does this compare with what is important to your team? If getting together is difficult for any reason, it may be best to have your team leader meet with the other team leader to learn more and report back. Then, stay connected with your key teams by communicating clearly and consistently. They, like you, are integral to the smooth and healthy functioning of your organization. Model what you seek from other teams by being approachable and sharing openly about your own team. Share how your team works and what is important to you.

Your team's performance is closely interconnected with all the other moving parts of your organization. The more your team understands this broader environment, the better. Like blood circulating freely through unblocked arteries and veins, the clearer the lines between your team and others, the smoother the whole system flows.

2 Win Confidence with Quality Work

The Rolling Stones have now played together for over 50 years, and over all these years, the Rock & Roll legends are known to meticulously rehearse for over 2 months before going on tour. They understand that after all these years, it's still a quality performance that wins over audiences—and perhaps only in this one way.

How others view your team from the outside looking in may legitimately be based on a medley of things, like team members' personality styles, humor, interests, and hobbies. But what ultimately marks your team's reputation is the quality of your work. This is what builds the trust and confidence others have in your team. By demonstrating a track record, other teams will know they can depend on you and what you can produce. Your team's reputation will be trusted to accomplish what it sets out to do, whether it's for customers, external stakeholders, colleagues, or other teams.

If others only had your team's work to go by, what would it say about your team? In other words, allow your work to speak for itself. Before your team's work is released, review it with fresh eyes. Ask your team members, "How will people outside our team see this work, and what will it say about us?"

External Relationship Strategies

Remind yourself and encourage your teammates not to be complacent. What The Rolling Stones have understood for more than five decades is that there is no substitute for quality performance. There is no better way to establish your team's presence and reputation than producing quality work.

3 Leverage Team Members' Relationship Strengths

One of the fastest ways to accelerate toward your team goals is to map out your team's relationship strengths. Shift your thinking away from allowing your team's natural people talents to surface "in the moment" or seeking them "as needed." Instead, chart them much like an org chart with names and strengths in each box. Your team can leverage these strengths with more intention.

According to research from MIT, here are three of the most common and impactful types of people who connect teams to the outside world. As you read about how they operate, see where you and others on your team fit the bill and how you might better make the most of your team's relationship strengths.

The first connector is the *ambassador*. Ambassadors are people who tend to be outgoing and know a wide range of people across teams, departments, and levels of the organization. When your team needs help or is looking to get something unique accomplished, ambassadors tend to know "just the right person." Ambassadors not only know a lot of people and build important relationships but also understand the unspoken cultural rules of the organization and the big picture needs of the company. On a food science development

191

team, the ambassador might be the scientist who constantly chats with the marketing team and therefore knows to connect your team's pitch for a new plant-based bag of chips to your company's selling goal of drawing in new types of consumers. More often than not, when you're looking to present to a key decision-maker, an ambassador can offer you insights into how and when to approach that person.

The second connector is the *scout*. Scouts will connect your team to the outside world. They don't have to be an extrovert. They don't need twenty years of experience, and they don't need to be best friends with the CEO. Scouts are people who bring important outside knowledge back to your team from the relationships they build and the information they gather. They attend conferences, read relevant new research, and spend time with specialists. Their passion for relevant subject matter motivates them to seek interesting conversations with people and bring new information to your group to help the whole team stay relevant. On a beverage system engineering team, a scout might be the engineer who is drawn to academic research around electrical engineering, keeps up with the latest literature, and attends conferences. When new technologies or solutions emerge that could apply to beverage systems, this person shares that information with their team to help keep the group competitive and ahead of the curve.

The third connector is the *coordinator*. Coordinators usually don't wield as much upward influence or external know-how as ambassadors, and they usually don't possess the specialized knowledge of a scout. "Coordinator" is often in their job title, and because their role is to coordinate, they are in constant communication with other teams, departments, and clients. The coordinator is the local touchpoint for questions or favors—both incoming and outgoing. Coordinators also tend to be skilled at recognizing the ripple effect your team's actions may have on another team. For instance, if end-of-the-month orders are going to come crashing into the warehouse, it's the sales coordinator who understands the process best and can give the warehouse the heads up for preparation and that extra appreciation for making it all happen or push back on the sales team from over-asking or breaking the order fulfillment process.

Talk together as a team about your relationship strengths and chart them. Does anyone have an important external relationship that doesn't fit one of these types? Name and assign other types that are valuable to your team's work. Include your team's leader for their formal connections and heightened influence with decision-makers, highly tenured people who have a vast historical and cultural understanding of the organization, or liaisons to specific people, teams, and organizations.

External Relationship Strategies

4 Communicate Clearly Outside the Team

Your team may know exactly what's going on with your work, but others outside your team may not understand and may need to understand earlier than you expect. Make external communication a regular topic on your team agendas. What do you need to communicate? To whom? When? As you figure this out, talk about how to best deliver your message so that it lands with the other team or person. Remember that the measurements, metrics, and vocabulary that are used every day on your team won't necessarily resonate clearly with people outside your team. Consider what you're saying from their perspective and adjust your messaging accordingly.

At a biotech company, a team of biochemists described communicating information across other teams as one of the most challenging aspects of their job (and these people are doing seriously complex work). In real time, a scientist must be able to communicate need-to-know information cross-functionally to improve their experiments. They have to effectively communicate the requirements of their science experiment to a computer programmer with no biology background. Then, they have to communicate to a hardware engineer how the hardware should function for the chemistry to work correctly.

This means taking highly complicated concepts and condensing them into understandable terms, often using metaphors in real time. This also means mastering a basic understanding of programming and software engineering to meet people halfway.

There's a lot to take away from this team's approach. Learn how to communicate the work that you do to other teams and learn the language of key teams that you interact with so that you can also meet them halfway. The delivery of a message can set a tone of respect and appreciation.

Here's how the biochemistry team does it: If you were to join this team, the first communication comes during your interview. They ask candidates to describe the science they worked on at their previous job as if they're speaking to a friend at a bar who knows nothing about science. The second ongoing communication effort is their weekly lab meeting. People go around the room updating the team on their part of the experiment. The team leader or more seasoned scientists will step in to correct language that isn't quite right. At the same time, though, they also push people to describe what they just said as if they were speaking to a software engineer, a programmer, or someone in marketing. This practice trains their scientists to adapt vocabulary to match their audience. The focus on communication is so intense and specific that it's almost like inventing and teaching a new language.

External
Relationship
Strategies

You don't want to hear, "Nobody gets what your team is up to." What the team of scientists does that your team can adopt and put to practice is this: They make communication important work.

Next time your team is deep in a priority or project that will eventually rely on people outside your team, step back and ask yourselves how you might talk about it, its progress, and your challenges to specific audiences outside your team. Doing so is part of your team's responsibility and will poise you to speak more clearly and concisely about your important work at any given moment. It will also build your connections with other teams and increase visibility for all that you do.

5 Build Bridges

The Golden Gate Bridge connects San Francisco to Marin County and spans nearly 9,000 feet. It's the world's biggest suspension bridge and is considered a Wonder of the Modern World. Sketches for the bridge began in 1921, construction started in 1933, and 4 years later, it opened to almost 8 million travelers annually. The bridge turned a limited system of ferries across the bay into a quick jaunt with a view. You can probably see where this is headed. Bridges, almost by definition, are worth the time and energy that they take to build. They are the quickest, most efficient way from Point A to Point B. For teams, social bridges connect your team to the vast nexus of people and resources around you. Bridges offer a direct line to other teams, departments, audiences, clients, headquarters, and organizations.

Just as it takes years of planning and construction to build a bridge, building a social bridge to your team requires time and deliberate effort. You have to consider who it makes sense for your team to get to know better, and then you have to take small, measured steps to make the actual connection.

Bridges can be built in many ways. You can invite someone in from a team you work closely with to ask for their perspective and learn more about how your work and their

External
Relationship
Strategies

work intersect. You can do someone a favor or offer a helpful perspective to them. You can even ask someone else for a favor. As long as you are careful to be respectful in your request (you should genuinely need their expertise), a favor can be an excellent way to forge a new relationship. Studies show that when someone does you a favor, it actually makes them like you more, not less. That holds especially true when you show respect and gratitude for their expertise and knowledge.

Bridges can also almost build themselves. Whenever your team finds itself in touch with a new person or a new team, take the time to get to know that person better, to understand their role and goals within the organization, and to draw out the connection between the work they do and the work your team does. Make that person feel welcome and express that your team would love to collaborate in the future. A pleasant and impactful first interaction will set that person up to feel comfortable reaching out to you, and vice versa.

As your team continues to add and maintain bridges inside your organization and beyond, you will enjoy a variety of interesting, specialized people you can turn to when stuck, in need of help, or in search of perspective from another side.

6 Host Visitors as Guests

Do you know of a restaurant that doesn't have the greatest food, but it's still one of your favorite places because of how welcomed you feel when you go there? They remember details like your favorite table and what "the usual" means when you order. At the Waldorf Astoria Hotel in New York, the hospitality shown over 50 years by bellhop Jimmy Elidrissi made guests feel like they were at their home away from home. By greeting and talking with guests as they arrived, he got to know them and how they were feeling. He was known to send hot tea and lemon up to the rooms of people he learned weren't feeling well, along with a little card from Jimmy. Guests, including eight United States Presidents, came to like and remember him so much that they would ask for him by name upon arrival.

Feeling welcomed is a product of genuine small touchpoints the hospitality industry knows best. Making guests feel this way is thoughtfully planned, down to every interaction, to ensure that their guests want to return. Add this insight to your team EQ aspirations and take note: Your group can damage your reputation with visitors when they don't feel noticed or welcomed.

To attend to how your team interacts with other groups and people outside your team, first acknowledge together that

External Relationship Strategies

you will think of visitors to your team as your guests and follow through on your agreed-upon touchpoints. Next, plan your touchpoints with care. It's not just the one friendly team member's responsibility. Be genuine in your welcome by rotating who will cover each touchpoint. If one team member is too busy to be present and attentive this time around, another teammate can step in.

Here are ideas before, during, and after for welcoming your guests into the most commonly visited space: your team meeting.

Touchpoint 1 – Before Your Guest's Visit:

- **Perfect Your Invite List.** Check with the team to ensure the invite list is correct and complete. If your visitors are first-time visitors, learn their names and how to pronounce them in advance.

- **Prepare Your Guest and Provide Context.** Don't just schedule a meeting that your guest is not expecting. Reach out ahead of time to explain why your team wants to meet and what the desired outcomes for the visit are. Don't assume your guest knows the context. Send an agenda, what to expect during the meeting (cameras will be on, lunch will be provided, when they should arrive and expect to speak, etc.), and what they should be prepared with and ready to discuss.

Touchpoint 2 – During Your Guest's Visit:

- **Welcome Visitors with Greetings and Introductions.** If the relationship is not new, include a minute or two to greet your visitor and interact. If your visitor is new to some of the team, add several minutes to the agenda so everyone can introduce themselves, including your guest. Meeting virtually is no excuse not to welcome visitors as you would in person.

- **Manage Your Time and Stick to Your Agenda.** Your visitor's time is important. If the meeting requires adjustments, give your guest the choice to stay or return. Be mindful to stay on topic rather than squander the visit with topics the guest isn't prepared to address (or that aren't pertinent). Don't indulge in sidebar conversations and inside jokes while your guest is there, or slow down to include them.

- **Close the Meeting with Genuine Thanks.** Have one team member escort your guest to the door. If the visit is virtual, the team meeting host can say, "Team, let's pause here on our agenda and allow our guest to move on with their day." While waiting for the guest to leave, the team can be smiling, waving, and thanking them for coming. These 10–15 seconds avoid the awkward or curt feeling at the end of the virtual visit.

Touch Point 3 – After Your Guest's Visit:

- **Send a Note by Text or Email to Your Guest.** Thank them for their visit with a personal insight or specific outcome that shows you valued their visit.

Teams are inundated with meetings, and with so many interactions with representatives of other teams, it's understandable that your group might become numb to the importance of these finer details. If your team can plan a few touchpoints, your interactions with visitors will feel as genuine as you intend for them to be and will deepen your connections with them outside this one visit.

7 Deepen Bonds with Other Teams

In chemistry, bonds are forces that unite atoms. Atoms change and rearrange themselves to react, creating new compounds and molecules. These reactions make up matter and life as we know it. Without the bonding process, the world would be limited in its complexity—and we would not exist! Imagine singular atoms floating around, unable to interact to combine and create anything new.

Your organization's growth also depends on the bonds forged between teams. The way teams bounce off of one another and react plays a big role in growing the organization and its ability to deal with complexity. Siloed, your team will only have limited views of the greater organization and fewer connections available to you.

Find opportunities to get to know people on other teams better and build shared experiences with them to form deeper bonds. A strong bond will help you access knowledge your team doesn't currently have and offer potential help when you need it, and provide you with a broader understanding of how your organization works.

Many teams feel their objectives are naturally at odds with or too dissimilar to the work of another team to bother investing in any relationship. These feelings lead groups to avoid each

External
Relationship
Strategies

other, work around each other, or ignore each other. Whatever the current differences of opinions your groups have or unpleasant history you may share, developing bonds with their team members can help both your teams to overcome difficulties going forward. It just takes one of you to hit reset and start building a relationship.

Productive relationships and bonds between teams are built on personal respect and a willingness to support each other when needed. Get to know one another as individuals and learn about the other team's challenges, stressors, and sources of pride. This will set the stage for more effective collaboration.

To check on the strength of your bonds with another team, ask yourselves these questions:

- Do we know who the members of that team are? Do we know their names?

- Do they know all our names?

- Do we understand their responsibilities and where our team's responsibilities and theirs overlap?

- Do we understand the common challenges our teams face? How about their unique challenges?

- Have we ever received feedback from this other team and done something about it?

- Has that team ever asked us for anything? Would they say

we responded well and helped them?

- Have we ever asked them how we can support them better?

- Have we done anything to facilitate clearer communication?

If you are honest with yourselves and answer "no" to any of these questions, you know where you can start to deepen your bonds with this team. If you're thinking your team will be doing all the work, remember that connections result in more leverage and influence for your team. Making the first move and doing your part offers real payoffs. Plus, when another team feels supported, they are much more likely to invest in your team in return.

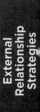

External
Relationship
Strategies

8 **Celebrate Bigger**

The last thing you want is for your victory celebration to make people who contributed to your victory resent or resist you. Imagine that your team just won a Timmy Award for Best Tech for Good because your work last year leveraged technology to make the world a better place. A select group of your team members attends the big event in Minneapolis to receive the coveted award. Everyone realizes there were many others who had a hand in this achievement.

It's understandable that there may be a core team who ultimately held the most responsibility for creating, developing, and executing a project, but who else had their hands in the mix? Consider the subject matter experts who may have been consulted and shared expert recommendations as well as processes and best practices. Consider the administrative support that often gets overlooked despite being essential to the project's success. When you consider all the people and teams who contributed, it's easy to see there's appreciation to share.

Celebrating the people outside your team who contributed to your achievement is a powerful way to build on your budding connections and show you care. You could communicate out that you want to thank the following other teams and people for their incredible contributions. Or, you could hold a breakfast in your team's part of the office with food, decorations, and signs thanking people who contributed. Or, you could celebrate offsite at a local establishment where everyone involved is thanked for a job well done. The point being, any form of celebration is better than letting helpful work go unnoticed.

Chances are, this won't be the only time you will need the input of these other teams and people. They will remember when they're appreciated, and they will certainly remember when they're not. Not to mention, positive emotions and bonding come naturally to a good celebration. Celebrate bigger when your team has a win, and everyone involved ultimately wins!

External
Relationship
Strategies

9 Increase Your Team's Visibility

When you do something well, and it makes you look good, people begin to see you as the angel and especially "good." In psychology, this is called the "halo effect." Your team's visibility within your organization works in a surprisingly similar way. If your team has a positive, organization-wide impact, even just once, you can set a precedent that casts a positive light on your team, opening you up to new relationships and opportunities.

How is visibility built? By learning about your organization's past and present, by being aware of current company goals and initiatives, by understanding how your team fits into this strategic picture, and by communicating with the right people at the right time in a careful and well-planned manner. Sound complicated? It is. And it requires your team to draw on all three of the other team EQ skills.

For example, a training department at a large nutrition company has been talking together for years about building out their training programs online. When the company announces that one of its new goals is to leverage technology across the organization, the team sees their opportunity and springs to action. They plan out a pitch connecting the online learning system directly to the company initiative, detailing how their training team is the best fit for the job. Their pitch, which they deliver to the Chief Learning Officer the week after she announces the technology-based goal, is perhaps unsurprisingly accepted. "Unsurprising" only because they did everything right, at the right time, and in the right way.

Like this training team, visibility usually isn't just a matter of luck. Together you have to identify company goals and motivations, usually by knowing the company's history and next priorities, drawing on well-connected teammates, and having conversations across departments. You also have to understand how your team supports the organization's mission and follow through so the team can earn its' stripes. Lean on your relationships and leverage the various strengths of people on your team. Then, as a group, seize opportunities as they come by taking a well-calculated risk and putting yourselves out there.

If you approach your collective efforts with care, you can succeed even when you fail, which is to say, you will gain other types of positive visibility even if your idea or contribution is rejected. Had the training team failed to win buy-in on their online learning system, they would have succeeded in connecting the work they do with the broader and deeper goals of their organization. That goes a long way with the people they pitched to, and it goes a long way in solidifying their own team's understanding of their relationship to other departments, teams, and key players.

It is important to mention that visibility doesn't always

have to involve a large initiative. Visibility can also be with one other person or team. If, for instance, your team's experience in customer service clues you into some specific customer needs and your team communicates those clearly to the marketing team, you may begin to forge a more influential relationship as that marketing team turns to you for future insights. Start thinking about your team's strategic place within the organization to ensure others are aware of your team's interests, capabilities, and accomplishments.

10 Take Matters into Your Own Hands

It's all too common for teams that are humming along on a project to suddenly find themselves at a standstill waiting on someone else to contribute one necessary piece. These moments, while seemingly inconsequential, can wreak more havoc than you might think. Besides slowing you down for a moment, they can halt your momentum and sap the life right out of your team's work. The solution to this problem is to learn *how* and *when* to take matters into your own hands. By taking steps of your own, your team can avoid feeling powerless and maintain your team's rhythm and positive drive.

Consider this example of how important momentum is to teams. In a study, two kinds of teams competed to build the tallest spaghetti tower: Teams of kindergarteners versus teams of MBA students. When the contest began, the MBA students brainstormed, worked through possible approaches, asked good questions, chose the approach they agreed would be most effective, and then assigned roles. Meanwhile, the kindergarteners just dove right in. They threw different pieces together to see how tall they could get the tower and said things like, "not there" or "do this." Time and again, teams of kindergarteners beat teams of MBA students, and by no slim margin either.

211

Kindergarteners averaged twenty-six-inch towers compared to the business students' mere ten.

The takeaway for teams is simple: Sometimes, action—and not getting too caught up in a plan—is the best way to get the results you need. Of course, not all work is as simple as building a tower of spaghetti. Most complex projects depend on more than one team for building and sustaining momentum. The question then becomes, *"When should we take matters into our own hands, and when shouldn't we?"* The answer is, only in two scenarios: after a standstill and before a deadline is missed.

For these scenarios, your team makes the offer to step in, awaits an answer, and watches the clock. Most teams receive an answer before having to weigh the pros and cons of taking over the task anyway. Consider things like necessary expertise or tools, as well as potential inter-team dynamics at your organization. If you do step in to get the job done, be sure to communicate early that you are doing so. This allows the other team to jump back in to join you side-by-side or to rise up and do their part. If they are simply unable to, they may also be sincerely grateful.

There will inevitably be projects and tasks where your team has to rely on others or other teams, and if that group fails you, grumbling about the other group isn't the way to go. Usually, it will be clear when your team can take the ball and run with it and when you need to sit back patiently to avoid role confusion. Either way, by weighing your options, you can do a lot to set your team at ease, knowing that you've done everything you can.

Keep it on your radar to consider those occasions where your team can easily step in, learn on the fly, and maintain everyone's momentum. Your team will quickly find a can-do attitude while reassuring the other team that this won't carry over to future projects and challenges without their knowledge or consent.

11 Avoid Pointing Fingers

This strategy should have the tagline: "How to not make a bad situation worse." Work is hard. We're all grownups, but it doesn't feel that way sometimes. Decisions were made too fast. Communication was poor. Sloppy errors slipped through. Deadlines got missed. Before you know it, hard feelings about broken promises or eroded trust show up, and the virtual meeting turns into a schoolyard. We revert to our 10-year-old selves, using the most sophisticated tactics we have from that time: we swiftly point a finger, so we won't be the one to get in trouble. As adults, we are expected to manage these difficult moments with ease, and yet when we're triggered, we revert and blame.

You may feel justified in the moment but regardless of the story or stakes, beware: When you blame people at work, you invite two destructive emotion monsters into the work culture, and both are hard to kick back out. The first is distraction. Everyone is focused on "who did it," and no one is fixing the problem or getting other work done. The second is shame. Mistakes on their own lead to embarrassment, but the public nature of blaming adds a toxic fuel to the fire. You've now made a bad situation so much worse, schoolyard-style. When the dust settles, your finger damaged the team's relationships and won't prevent the problem next time.

As a team, you can hit the pause button before the blame game begins. There is space and time to fill between an error made and the urge to blame. During your pause, here are better choices available to your group:

1. **Seek solace.** Instead of being quick to blame, be quick to talk openly and safely within your team. Get all of your thoughts, feelings, and perspectives clear. If you need to vent, check out Emotion Management Strategy 7 (Go Ahead and Vent, Briefly and with Purpose) for how to get that out of your system.

2. **Stick to "what" and "how;" let go of the "who."** Focus on the facts of the problem and how it happened, both of which can inform possible solutions. Take notes so you can grow a list of contributing factors with others later. No names allowed. Focusing on the "who" will take you back down the path toward blame. It will require some discipline, but it is a healthier habit to form.

3. **Find lessons that your team can learn.** Review your facts list and discuss what lessons there are for your team specifically. Looking at your part first can redirect your attention away from blaming and solidify your team's approach toward future blunders.

4. **Decide on your team's end game.** What do you want your

team to be known for? In other words, what do you want your team's reputation to be? The team that brings people together in a crisis or drives a wedge between groups? The team that is the first to point a finger or the first to point to next steps? Really stop and think about this. Clarifying your vision together can extinguish the urge to blame.

5. **Engage outward.** When the problem is in the rear-view mirror, engage the other team thoughtfully and with respect. This might be an all-hands meeting with both teams or a smaller meeting with one or two members from each team. This is your opportunity to share what you learned, including how you felt, and ask the other team to share the same. Be part of the solution. In the end, when teams are willing to actively seek solutions to problems together, rather than cast blame, it's a moment to build trust instead of barriers.

6. **If the "who" is inevitable.** If, during this process, you realize that "the who" is a critical piece to an error, allow for the team leader to handle it in a smaller, private setting. Corrective action is not your team's job.

Your team should not put blinders on or sweep issues under the rug. Issues and mistakes happen and pausing the blame game to learn about what led to those mistakes, instead of pointing at the "who," will help your team, as adults, manage errors with ease.

12 Own Your Mistakes

Owning a mistake is like fixing a leak by repairing the roof instead of just putting out empty pots. You may dread having to do it, and it might feel like more work and costly work, but it's worth it. Your problem won't continue to get worse.

From the moment your team makes a mistake, other people and teams may feel annoyed. This is the small leak in your relationships. If left unattended, annoyance can widen to feelings of resentment and mistrust. As time passes, your relationship will become more difficult to repair. Alternatively, by owning a team mistake early on, your group will usually be met with appreciation for the courage it took, which actually builds trust with those impacted.

Consider this example at a busy, high-end Persian restaurant with a constant influx of customers. One night, the chef and his team mix up several orders over the course of just a couple of hours. They overcook one meal, undercook another, and get a third completely wrong. Customers send their food back, and the waiting staff team feels the brunt of the disappointed, hangry customers. Servers are the ones who deal with the consequences of the kitchen staff's mistakes.

Hardworking kitchen crews could brush off these mistakes as "the best they could do," but this restaurant's kitchen crew

External Relationship Strategies

(the head chef, sous chef, line cooks, and kitchen assistant) took pride in both their cooking and in working smoothly with their wait staff. The first thing the crew did was to send the head chef or sous chef to the tables that received a mistake. Here, a personal apology reassured the table that the corrected meal would soon arrive. They didn't stop there and scheduled a quick huddle with the wait staff right before opening the next day. They apologized for what they understood to be a tough previous night and briefly explained their plan for preventing future mistakes or at least catching them prior to sending them to the tables.

Team EQ is not about becoming perfect, as mistakes do happen. It's about what your group does after a mistake is made. Panicking, shifting blame, brushing it off, or trying to cover it up all create leaks in your team relationships. So why do teams spend energy on so many ways of making things worse rather than the one true thing that will make it better? Fear. Fear of someone flying off in a rage at what you've done. Fear of losing status. Fear of being perceived as the team that produces poor quality or can't be trusted. Even unspoken feelings of hope that if deflection works, maybe no one will notice or remember the mistake and your team will have slipped by unscathed. The trouble is your team becomes the emperor with no clothes. Everyone sees and knows about your mistake, and now they are wondering: *Does your team not see it, or won't see it? Does your team not have the courage to acknowledge it?* These are more costly leaks than even the mistake itself.

Owning a mistake openly costs much less and earns more social capital for your team than you realize. In addition to the respect, compassion, and appreciation you might gain, your group has now modeled the type of team EQ behavior you would expect in return. The wait staff sees the cooking crew's transparency and accountability and feels empowered to replicate it when they make a mistake. Just like that, the chef and his team created a restaurant environment where teams are accountable and communicative with each other and with customers.

One last word of team EQ advice. When a teammate makes a mistake (say, for example, the dinner errors were made by one new line cook), it impacts the team's reputation as a unit. That doesn't mean the team should single that teammate out. Demonstrate that you have each other's backs by presenting a united front to outsiders when taking responsibility for errors. Owning your mistakes as a group will solidify your reputation as a cohesive unit in the eyes of other teams as well as in the eyes of your own team.

External Relationship Strategies

13 Frame Requests to the Mission

Enthusiasm and support within your team won't always equate to enthusiasm and support from those outside your team. To increase your chances of winning people's interest and the resources you need, frame your requests to your organization's mission.

At their very core, missions are emotional appeals, a purpose valued by everyone that reminds people why the work you do together is worthwhile. Missions energize and inspire, so use yours to your team's advantage. Connect your requests to the mission to help decision makers see what you see and to feel inspired by what inspires you.

Here's what the process of winning buy-in looks like in action. A leadership team at a hospital is trying to make the much-needed switch from tracking patients' charts on computers to a new software capable of being carried around on a tablet. The leadership team is elated. Tablets will help the organization transform digitally! After months of motivated, late nights, they announced the initiative to the hospital, only to feel shocked as their announcement is met with silence and blank stares, even slight resistance. To their medical teams, the tablets sounded like a nuisance. They were high-performing teams already, and this change meant taking more valuable time out of a packed schedule to learn how to manage the same information. The lack of enthusiasm was tangible, negativity spreading through the hospital's introductory Q&A sessions.

The leadership team reconvened to change not their solution but their entire message. They imagined how people use tablets and looked for specific connections to the mission: We provide the best, personalized care. The tablets would finally untether staff from machines and allow them to sit and face their patients as they talk together, rather than typing and talking behind a wall-mounted computer station. Access to important patient data remains immediate and now portable, updated by each patient care team member in real time. By shifting their messaging toward "a patient-centered improvement," the leadership team made it possible for staff from all professions to see the why behind the required time and training. Staff adapted and did so enthusiastically. The leadership team even found that teams began to offer feedback and further ideas on how the tablets could best be leveraged.

This strategy can and should start much sooner than it did for this hospital's leadership team. As you or your teammates come up with ideas that require resources, approval, or implementation beyond the bounds of your team, get in the habit of connecting those ideas back to the organization's mission. Ask

External
Relationship
Strategies

yourselves, why does this matter to the organization, the people who will be involved, and the customers our mission serves?

By making this strategy a habit, you will naturally begin to weave your team's work and its needs into the fabric of the organization. Other people and teams will find your work and ideas more compelling, and you will likely win new friends and allies for future work.

14 **Tackle a Wider Problem**

It might be surprising to learn who stepped forward to partner and guide this initiative for Little Rock, Arkansas.

Rock It! Lab is a business incubator program for aspiring business owners who don't have the resources they need to get started. The goal is to turn an idea into a profitable company capable of scaling operations and contributing to economic growth in Central Arkansas. The lab is housed on three floors in a 125-year-old warehouse in the River Market District, and each floor will serve a different function. Entrepreneurs will have access to sewing machines, a screen printer, embroidery equipment, open space, meeting areas, and mentorship to encourage collaboration, as well as a retail area to feature and sell the goods they create. It's a modern work environment at no charge.

The community team that stepped up was the Central Arkansas Library. Two years prior, the Central Arkansas Library System had hosted a community meeting to reignite interest in available library services. A local entrepreneur, Benito Lubazibwa, stepped forward with the idea to partner with the library on supporting people whose "hopes and dreams die in the bank parking lot." In turn, the library recognized how closely the partnership aligned with its longtime mission of educating and informing the community. Now, the lab's goal is to graduate 100 entrepreneurs annually, filling a hole in the city's entrepreneurial ecosystem. They also succeeded in reigniting interest in library services.

Your team can also tackle a wider problem in the ecosystem where you operate by leaning on your relationships outside your team. Working with people or teams, you might not typically consider will grow your group's ability to flex the boundaries of your work to a wider arena. Why not be the ones to bring forward your team's interest in directly addressing a larger organizational problem? Other teams or stakeholders may need a moment to think bigger or farther down the road, so allow for that time if you need them to join the effort. They will also appreciate your group taking the initiative to start the conversation. Projects like these are filled with complexity and unknowns, so get ready to leverage all four of your group's team EQ skills to make the changes you want to see in the world.

EPILOGUE

Team emotional intelligence may sound like a new topic related to emotional intelligence, but it's been researched and written about for decades. Early work on the study of group dynamics dates back to the 1930s. A 1932 study at Columbia showed that teams of four outperformed individuals at problem-solving. The advantage teams offered was social interaction. As team members went back and forth problem-solving, incorrect suggestions were rejected by the group 75% of the time. Individuals, on the other hand, caught their own errors only 25% of the time.

A 1952 study demonstrated another kind of social support that group interactions offer during problem-solving. Alone, an individual begins to problem solve tentatively. They tend to question their first thoughts. Uncertainty introduces anxious feelings which block their ability to free associate, to finish out the idea, or to find new ideas. A group can offer support to a team member with a half-baked idea through encouraging gestures (like nodding, smiling, and listening intently). This support reassures the team member's anxiety and frees their mind from the interruption.

From the 1970s studies into the early 2000s, the body of research on the influence of emotions on team performance continued to expand, and it coincided with Daniel Goleman introducing the concept of emotional intelligence to the business world. In 2004, Travis Bradberry and I developed the Emotional Intelligence Appraisal® - Team Edition to help team members measure their group's team EQ behaviors. These assessment results allow teams to see how well their group applies the four essential team EQ skills on the job.

The field of team EQ research is still flourishing with the following new discoveries and evolving insights.

Virtual, Remote, and Hybrid Teamwork

The human brain doesn't change drastically with each new generation or century. That said, our understanding of our brains and how we use them and care for them is expanding rapidly. We know, for instance, that areas in the brain adapt to environmental stressors, injury, or disease in remarkable ways. We also understand that neural connections grow and strengthen through repetition and use, just as our muscles grow and strengthen with increasing and repeated use. Your team's we-radar is strengthened through repeated inter-actions sensed by the mirror neurons in each team member's brain as you watch, listen, react, and talk to each other. At the same time, neglect or disuse can weaken social muscles through the inattention or multi-tasking that technology devices allow.

> **Neglect or disuse can weaken social muscles through the inattention or multi-tasking that technology devices allow.**

Teams dipped their toes into virtual team communications during the 2010s, and by December of 2019, the video conference tool Zoom had about 10 million users. It was the social distancing response to the Covid-19 pandemic in early 2020 that pushed teams into the deep end of virtual and remote teamwork. By May 2020, Zoom had more than 300 million users. Teams today continue to figure out how to optimize virtual and hybrid teamwork using multiple technology platforms.

It's early to make definitive conclusions about the impact virtual and hybrid teamwork will have on managing emotions and relationships. It's also too early to conclude definitively on the impact that processing emotions and cultivating relationships virtually will have on virtual and hybrid team performance. Your attention is on your devices, and your eyes and ears are straining to read how team members feel on a screen with some number between 3 and 30 heads gazing at you. Your mirror neurons are used in a different way for hours a day. You and your teammates are working harder mentally and emotionally to compensate for what would be your minds' natural ability to send and receive clear communication between each of you.

Five factors contributing to videoconferencing fatigue are being explored by researchers. Each influences the emotion data being absorbed and interpreted by your team as you meet virtually. The first three create fatigue through overload: Excessive amounts of eye gaze, increased self-evaluation from staring at your own image, and the extra focus on fewer cues. The second creates fatigue through constraints: Lack of physical mobility and the collapse from sensing emotions in a three-dimensional environment to sensing them in a two-dimensional environment.

Remote communication platforms narrow the range and subtlety of emotion expressions that your mirror neurons detect automatically when you are in the same room with people. The way video calls place everyone in central view is a kind of brain blast that overloads your mind. This view doesn't allow you to focus on one person at a time with others in your peripheral view the way you might in person. If you select the speaker-only view, then you eliminate that valuable peripheral information. You don't see full body postures when heads are reduced to small squares, and your eyes may miss micro-expressions on your teammates' faces. A twitch in the eye or eyebrow area or slight movements near the mouth make a big difference in your perception. Even with audio-only conference calls, you've likely experienced increased difficulty with managing who should speak first after a question and evaluating natural pauses in the conversation.

What does all this mean for you and others working on virtual and hybrid teams? In his book *Social Intelligence*, Daniel Goleman discussed the importance of balancing the efficient communication that technology enables with nurturing in-person interactions and relationships. Teams can choose to value this insight and put to use what you've learned in this book. Value your team relationships as a guiding light, and generally head in the direction that invests in the team's emotion and relationship skills. You can do this virtually or in person, and it's going to require effort.

Value your team relationships as a guiding light, and generally head in the direction that invests in the team's emotion and relationship skills.

Virtual teamwork success will require your team to weigh the pros and cons related to face-to-face, phone, and screen interactions and in what proportion. It may include revisiting unspoken norms between listeners and speakers on screen. In person, looking away or getting up from your chair may mean you're being rude to the speaker. On screen, it may be important to break the mental and emotional load from stares and to physically move about. Every team can discuss these matters and try out how the strategies in this book can be adjusted for videoconferencing, conference calls, and in-person settings.

How Your Own EQ Contributes to Team EQ

If you are a reader who is new to the term "emotional intelligence" and if you are now asking what is it exactly, the answer is, a powerful and practical skill set. The physical source of emotional intelligence (EQ) is the two-way communication between rational thoughts located in the frontal lobe and emotions signaling from the limbic system of the brain. When a person with a high EQ encounters people and situations throughout their day, they notice how they feel, understand what triggers their reactions and why (self-awareness), and constructively manage their words and actions in response (self-management). They notice and empathize with how other people are feeling (social awareness), and take the time to build, deepen, or repair relationships in their social network (relationship management).

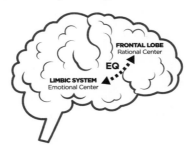

Developing emotional intelligence does not mean you ignore your emotions so you can be entirely rational. It also doesn't mean you learn to ignore your logical side so you can be solely emotional. People need both their instinctual feelings and their constructive thoughts to achieve their goals and face life's challenges.

Does increasing your EQ help you become a better teammate? Yes, it certainly does. Handling your own emotions constructively as you work with your teammates is a big help to them. Doing your part to develop healthy one-to-one relationships with the people on your team contributes to your team's performance. Discover

Doing your part to develop healthy relationships with the people on your team contributes to your team's performance.

your own EQ skill levels in the book *Emotional Intelligence 2.0* and find EQ strategies there that will help you achieve success and well-being, even on your most challenging days.

Team EQ Norms

Team norms are one of many team strategies (actions your team can put into practice) to help your group strengthen your emotion management and relationship skills. When agreements are made up front for how to work together, and there is buy-in about what is expected from team members, there are fewer surprises, disappointments, frustrations, or irritations between team members. Your team will have fewer negative emotions to manage.

A research team lead by Vanessa Urch Druskat and Peter Wolff studied which team norms specifically propel group emotional intelligence. The norms they've studied address team EQ behaviors at the individual, group, and organizational levels. If you'd like a suggested set, supported by their research, the following five team norms will help your team operate more effectively within and across team boundaries:

1. **Continually build an understanding of each other,** so team members feel known and understood.

2. **Continually re-evaluate the status-quo** to include team-level strengths, needs, preferences, and resources.

3. **Continually plan ahead and think proactively** when problems occur, rather than rigidly or reactively.

4. **Continually seek information from the larger organization** to understand the needs, preferences, perspectives, and behaviors of important people and teams outside the team.

5. **Engage and work with colleagues outside the team** to acquire information, resources, and support.

A sixth norm, confronting teammates who break norms, was not supported by their research. They couldn't confirm whether team members had the skills to confront each other without making things worse. The researchers wrote, "Providing difficult feedback, even if it is constructive so that it can be heard without harming members' sense of safety, is not easy and must be skillfully done. Throughout the study, team leaders reported to the researchers that their teams were uncomfortable giving each other feedback."

The Future of Teamwork

The research in the area of teamwork is burgeoning with questions. How will we use virtual, remote, and hybrid team communication to engage, innovate, or create cultures of inclusion? How does technology limit or facilitate teams dealing with their emotions and relationships? A novel approach to this area of study is the use of robots on teams. How can robots help groups working together to better recognize and manage emotions? How can they influence group emotions to positively impact performance?

One 2015 study looked at how a robot teammate can intervene to moderate conflict. Researchers asked 53 teams to troubleshoot an urgent problem in 10 minutes. Each team was made up of three humans and a robot. One human on each team was a carefully trained actor, and they expressed one of two trigger statements as the team worked together. One trigger statement was directed with frustration at the task ("That's not a good idea," or "I wouldn't do that"), and the other was directed with frustration at one of the other team members ("You're moving too slow," or "You're not very good at this."). To start the personal attack, the actor said, "You're stupid," to grab the team's attention.

In immediate response to personal triggers, the robot attempted a repair comment such as, "Whoa man, that was inappropriate. Let's stay positive," or "Dude, what the heck! Let's stay positive." The robot also made positive comments using "we-mindset" language. Examples included "We could try. . . ," or "I really want us to solve this in time." The study found that these more colloquial statements injected humor (surprise at the robot's casual language), alleviated tension, and often sparked laughter during the interactions. One person commented, "It doesn't like you." Another said, "Haha, the robot thought you were inappropriate." The most common response was an exchange of looks and nervous laughter.

The research team expected to find that the robot's comments would reduce the team's perceptions of conflict. The study found the exact opposite. These teams showed higher perceptions of conflict. The researchers offered one possible explanation. The robot pointing out the personal attack announced there was a team violation and made it more powerful, increasing awareness of the conflict.

When the researchers reviewed the videos of the teams working, they watched participants glance over to the actor to see if they would respond to the robot or apologize. After no apology or response, team members immediately suggested next actions, as though they would rather get back to work than engage with the conflict. In effect, the robot made sure the team violation wasn't ignored, but the team still didn't deal with it.

Research shows that suppressing conflict can negatively

impact team performance. Stifling the expression of negative feelings over time has been shown to have negative consequences for a person's health and personal relationships. The robot increased team awareness of conflict, but the conditions necessary to get team members to engage in resolving conflict remain unclear. Perhaps a team that is actively aware of and practicing team emotional intelligence strategies might be better equipped to respond to a robot's call-out and resolve their conflict.

In a study where mixed robot and human teams played cards, robots that expressed we-mindset phrases ("We are the best!" Or "We were not so good this time.") were rated as more likable and trustworthy than robots that express phrases that are I-based ("I am impressed with your move!" Or "I played incredibly well!). This research helps us learn how to facilitate positive feelings among team members (using the "we-mindset") and how to moderate negative feelings that impact a team's behavior and relationships (calling out and resolving conflict). Even if robots don't join our teams, we are already learning from them about how to best spread positivity and best manage negativity.

Ongoing Trends and Research Findings

For this book, the team at TalentSmartEQ translated what team research findings mean for teams looking to put behavioral science into practice. Trends and research findings will continue to shape our understanding of team emotional intelligence as well as yours. We invite you to stay in touch with us to continue learning. Discoveries from the body of EQ research, team EQ research, and TalentSmartEQ's applied research are available on our website to encourage continued conversations and insights. To access trends for teams working in specific industries and other interesting EQ topics, please visit: www.talentsmarteq.com/eqtrends.

To access ongoing trends and other interesting topics, visit our website at talentsmarteq. com/eqtrends.

Closing Thoughts

Team members can do a lot to contribute to the health and performance of the teams they are invited to join. Many ideas and team EQ strategies in this book offer insights and guidance for when to speak up, when to check in with a teammate, and when it may be best to say nothing at all. There's also a limit to how much one team member can do on their own.

Team EQ is a collective effort, a journey to be taken together. Rather than allowing your group's emotions and relationships to determine how much your team can accomplish, venture to understand and use team EQ skills and strategies to your team's advantage. To harness the full power of your team's potential, introduce every team member to the four essential team EQ skills and prepare yourselves for this group adventure. Strive for peak team performance by adding the management of your team's emotions and relationships to the ways in which you excel. With deliberate practice, your team emotional intelligence skills will elevate the work you already engage in every day and help your team summit the peaks on your horizon.

DISCUSSION QUESTIONS FOR READING GROUPS AND TEAMS

———

Discussing the following team emotional intelligence questions with others will help you begin to contribute to the performance of teams you will join or are a part of now. If your discussion group is your team, use these questions to start a meaningful conversation and to build your understanding of how the four essential team EQ skills apply to your current team goals.

1. How many members in your group were familiar with the term "emotional intelligence" before reading *Team Emotional Intelligence 2.0*?

2. For those who were unfamiliar with emotional intelligence, what's the most important thing you discovered after reading *Team Emotional Intelligence 2.0*?

3. For those who were already familiar with emotional intelligence, what's the most important thing you discovered about how emotions influence teamwork?

4. Have you or your group experienced anything like the Cathedral Peak climbers? Have you ever noticed early warning signs to a failed team project but ignored them in the early stages? Or, have you ever overlooked your feelings or other perspectives, only to regret doing so later on? Share your story.

5. What behaviors emerge when emotions take over on your team? An example might be "everyone interrupts each other" or "a few members dominate the conversation."

6. What's one experience that stands out in your memory that describes how your team handles feelings?

7. What are you most proud of when it comes to how your team connects with each other? How does your team connect with other teams or people outside your team?

8. Is there anything covered in the book that will help you in the next six months? How about next week?

9. How are team EQ skills visible in current events today? Discuss sports teams, school groups, teams that produce new products, teams that solve community problems,

groups taking on scientific challenges, and any other groups that come to mind.

10. Can you think of any historical groups or events that were influenced by either poor team EQ skills or excellent team EQ skills?

11. Which team EQ skill (emotion awareness, emotion management, internal relationships, external relationships) do you think is strongest for your team? What made you choose that skill?

12. Which team EQ skill do you think is weakest for your team? Which strategies could you practice to strengthen this skill? How would it benefit your performance?

13. Which relationship strengths among your team members can you leverage better?

14. What will make practicing team EQ skills challenging for your group? How might you address these challenges before they become barriers to making progress?

15. Three themes emerge time and again in the comments section of team emotional intelligence assessments. Take a close look below, considering your own team's dynamics. Discuss how these themes apply or don't apply on your team.

- "One or a few members dominate my team."

- "Go directly to the person you have a problem with. I don't want to hear about it!"

- "We set our feelings aside to get work done. There's not really a place for emotions at work on this team."

16. What would you like to share with the other people on your team? Ask them about their views too.

   - How do you feel as a member of the team? Do you feel valued and respected?

   - What do you notice about the team handling emotions when you all are together?

   - How do you manage your own emotions at team meetings?

   - Who on the team do you want to get to know better?

   - Which relationships outside the team (people or other teams) do you want to invest in further?

ACKNOWLEDGMENTS

We are extremely grateful to our writing team and colleagues at TalentSmartEQ for their collaboration, wisdom, and contributions. We like to think of this book itself as testament to the multiplicative powers of a collaborative team. In particular, thank you to Sue DeLazaro for her editing eye, advice, and ideas for improving the design of the team EQ skills and process models. She was always there as a sounding board as we considered the tough questions.

The following subject matter experts contributed strategies for the book and offered invaluable feedback and insights along the way: Josh Rosenthal, David Brzozowski, Howard Farfel, and Sheri Duchock. Thank you to Amy Miller for combing through and theming thousands of team emotional intelligence comments and to Cecilia Ngan for preparing data files for this process. Thank you to Kendrick Wong, Josh Rosenthal, and Sue DeLazaro for collaborating with us on the original set of team EQ strategies.

Thank you to Travis Bradberry for his early research and believing in EQ from the beginning, and for codeveloping the Emotional Intelligence Appraisal – Team Edition.

A special thank you to the team who designed the book: Kate Barsby and Taryn McKenzie for their marketing expertise, Desmond Hardy for designing graphic images, and Tingting Naggiar for her excellent graphic design and layout of the book, and Sue Stevenson at Lifted Fog Photography and Kate Barsby for photos.

Appreciation must also be sent to the team at Ingram who have provided support, guidance, and distribution for this third TalentSmartEQ book.

And lastly, thank you to all of our "TalentSmarties" for all of your support and encouragement along the way, and for bringing team emotional intelligence to the world.

Finally, we feel heartfelt appreciation for our families for their patience, inspiration, and support while we wrote through days, evenings, and weekends. Thank you, Greg, Claire, and Ingrid. Thank you, Emily Browne for being such a clever, brilliant, and broad-sweeping first reader. Thank you Johnny Cappetta, Daniel Goulden, Jay Loscar, and Mohammad Hakima for teaching me so much about writing and for always making writing fun. Thank you Jeannine, Jeff, Katie, and Monty for always reading and for always keeping it real.

NOTES

Peak Performance

Laurence Gonzales, *Deep Survival: Who Lives, Who Dies and Why* (New York: W. W. Norton & Company, 2005); Nick Wilder, "Cathedral Peak Rock Climbing," Mountain Project, posted June 22, 2006, https://www.mountainproject.com/area/105835696/cathedral-peak. The story of the Cathedral Peak climb is fictionalized from a true event discussed by Gonzales. The description, "It's a great big lightning rod," came from Wilder's post.

John Muir, *My First Summer in the Sierra*, (Boston and New York: Houghton Mifflin Company, 1911), chap. 10, "The Tuolumne Camp," http://vault.sierraclub.org/john_muir_exhibit/writings/my_first_summer_in_the_sierra.aspx. John Muir's sketch of Cathedral Peak can be found in this chapter. The book is in the public domain and can be accessed for free on the Sierra Club website.

Team Emotional Intelligence: Why It Matters

Jeanette Nyden, Kate Vitasek, and David Frydlinger, *Getting to We: Negotiating Agreements for Highly Collaborative Relationships*, (New York: Palgrave Macmillan, 2013), "The Power of We" pp. 207–214. You can learn more about the "we-mindset" and "we-radar" in this chapter.

World Economic Forum, *Future of Jobs Report* (2020). EQ rankings as an in-demand future skillset can be found in this report.

Dan Goleman, *Emotional Intelligence: Why It Can Matter More Than IQ*, (New York: Bantam, 2005). Dan Goleman introduced emotional intelligence to the world in this book.

Jack Mayer and Peter Salovey, "The Intelligence of Emotional Intelligence," *Intelligence* 17 (1993), pp. 433–442. John D. Mayer and Alexander Stevens, "An Emerging Understanding of the Reflective (Meta) Experience of Mood," *Journal of Research in Personality* 28 (1994), pp. 351–373. Emotional intelligence research linking emotional intelligence to success includes these two articles.

Marjorie Shaw, "A Comparison of Individuals and Small Groups in the Rational Solution of Complex Problems," *The American Journal of Psychology* 44, no. 3 (1932), pp. 491–504.

Shaw researched how small groups outperformed individuals on problem-solving tasks.

Travis Bradberry and Jean Greaves, *Emotional Intelligence 2.0* (San Diego: TalentSmart, Inc., 2004); Travis Bradberry and Jean Greaves, *Emotional Intelligence Appraisal – Team Edition* (San Diego: TalentSmart, 2004). TalentSmartEQ reached over 2 million learners with this book and assessment.

Edward. F. Pace-Schott et al., "Physiological Feelings," *Neuroscience and Biobehavioral Reviews* 103 (2019), pp. 267–304; Cynthia Fisher, "Mood and Emotion while Working: Missing Pieces of Job Satisfaction?," *Journal of Organizational Behavior* 21, no. 2 (2000), pp. 185–202. Emotions, feelings, and moods are discussed by Pace-Schott et al. and Fisher.

Sourya Acharya and Samarth Shukla, "Mirror Neurons: Enigma of the Metaphysical Modular Brain," *Journal of Natural Science, Biology and Medicine* 3, no. 2 (2012), pp. 118; Hyeonjin Jeon and Seung-Hwan Lee, "From Neurons to Social Beings: Short Review of the Mirror Neuron System Research and Its Socio-Psychological And Psychiatric Implications," *Clinical Psychopharmacology and Neuroscience* 16, no. 1 (2018), pp.18–31. Mirror neurons' important role is discussed in these two articles.

Infei Chen, "Brain Cells for Socializing: Does an Obscure

Nerve Cell Help Explain What Gorillas, Elephants, Whales—and People—Have in Common?," *Smithsonian Magazine* (June 2009), https://www.smithsonianmag.com/science-nature/brain-cells-for-socializing-133855450/. Chen discusses spindle neurons' special role.

Patrick Hof, "The Social Neuron," February 27, 2015 at the World Science Festival, https://www.youtube.com/watch?v=MXZ3YPl5Rmw. Hof, a neuroscientist, discusses Spindle cells and the social brain.

Ralph Adolphs, "The Social Brain," presented February 20, 2013, as a TedXCaltech Talk. https://www.youtube.com/watch?v=nPj01uzRHY0. Adolphs, a Caltech professor, discusses large-scale collaborative behavior.

Mathew Lieberman, "The Social Brain and Its Superpowers," presented October 7, 2013, as a TEDxStLouis talk, https://www.youtube.com/watch?v=NNhk3owF7RQ. Lieberman, a UCLA professor, discusses how our brains are wired to be connected, how we need other humans to survive infancy, and how social pain is real pain.

David Despain, "Early Humans Used Brain Power, Innovation and Teamwork to Dominate the Planet," *Scientific American*, (February 2020). Despain discusses social achievements in this article.

Tony Reichhardt, "Twenty People Who Made Apollo Happen," Air & Space, June 7, 2019, https://www.airspacemag.com/airspacemag/twenty-people-who-made-apollo-happen-180972374/. See this article for information on the people who made the Apollo mission happen.

Harold G. McCurdy and Wallace E. Lambert, "The Efficiency of Small Human Groups in the Solution of Problems Requiring Genuine Cooperation," *Journal of Personnel* 20 (1952), pp. 478–94.

Sigal G. Barsade, "The Ripple Effect: Emotional Contagion and Its Influence on Group Behavior," *Administrative Science Quarterly* 47, no. 4 (2002), pp. 644–675. In this article, Barsade discusses the transfer of moods among team members.

Irving L. Janis, Groupthink: *Psychological Studies of Policy Decisions and Fiascoes* (Boston: Cengage Learning, 1982). Janis discusses positive feelings' potential to lead to negative results.

Lutz Kaufmann and Claudia Wagner, "Affective Diversity and Emotional Intelligence in Cross-Functional Sourcing Teams," *Journal of Purchasing and Supply Management* 23, no. 1 (2017), pp. 5–16; Christina Arfara and Irene Samanta, "The Impact of Emotional Intelligence on Improving Team-Working: The Case of Public Sector (National Centre for Public Administration and Local Government – N.C.P.A.L.G.)," *Procedia – Social and Behavioral Sciences* 230 (2016), pp. 167–175; Azadeh Rezvania and Pouria Khosravi, "Emotional Intelligence: The Key to Mitigating Stress and Fostering Trust among Software Developers Working on Information System Projects," *International Journal of Information Management* 48 (2019), pp.139–150; Jordi Quoidbach and Michel Hansenne, "The Impact of Trait Emotional Intelligence on Nursing Team Performance and Cohesiveness," *Journal of Professional Nursing* 25 (2009), pp. 23–29; Gretchen Machta, David Nembhard, and Robert Leicht, "Operationalizing Emotional Intelligence for Team Performance," *International Journal of Industrial Ergonomics* 71 (2019), pp. 57–63. These studies discuss the link between team emotional intelligence and various performance outcomes.

Gloria Barczak, Felicia Lassk, and Jay Mulki, "Antecedents of Team Creativity: An Examination of Team Emotional Intelligence, Team Trust, and Collaborative Culture," *Creativity and Innovation Management* 19 (2010), pp. 332–345; Sam R. Wilson, William C Barley, Louisa Ruge-Jones, and Marshall Scott Poole, "Tacking amid Tensions: Using Oscillation to Enable Creativity in Diverse Teams," *Journal of Applied Behavioral Science* (2020). These articles discuss team EQ, diversity, and creativity.

The Four Essential Skills: What Team EQ Looks Like

Travis Bradberry and Jean Greaves, *The Emotional Intelligence Quick Book* (New York: Simon & Schuster, 2005).

The Pathway to Team EQ: Your Action Plan

Maxwell Maltz, Psycho Cybernetics, *A New Way to Get More Living Out of Life* (New York: Pocket Books, 1960). Dr. Maltz introduced the "21/90" rule in this book.

Hayes, John R. "Cognitive processes in creativity." In *Handbook of creativity* (Boston: Springer, 1989), pp. 135-145. Hayes, a Carnegie Mellon psychologist, introduced the "rule of 100" and "10-year rule" in this paper.

Phillippa Lally, Cornelia van Jaarsveld, Henry Potts, and Jane Wardle, "How Are Habits Formed: Modeling Habit Formation in the Real World," *European Journal of Social Psychology* 40, no. 6 (2009), pp. 998-1009. This research examined the variability of time habit-forming. The volunteers with the most consistent daily practice reached 95% automaticity in 18 to 254 days.

Emotion Awareness Strategies

Craig Foster, *My Octopus Teacher*, directed by Pippa Ehrlich and James Reed (False Bay, South Africa: Netflix, 2020), https://www.netflix.com/title/81045007. "Strategy #2, Check In on One Another," discusses this documentary,

Mandalit Del Barco, "Simone Biles Highlights the Unique Stresses Athletes Feel at the Tokyo Olympics," NPR, July 28, 2021. https://www.npr.org/sections/tokyo-olympics-live-updates/2021/07/28/1021670837/simone-biles-tokyo-olympics-mental-health. "Strategy #9, Get to Know Your Team Under Stress," discusses the stress Biles experienced.

Emotion Management Strategies

Debra Nelson and James Campbell Quick, *Organizational Behavior: Foundations, Realities and Challenges*, third edition (Cincinnati: West Publishing, 1994). "Strategy #2, Focus on Health Reactions to Change," discusses behavioral reactions to change covered in this book.

Barbara Wild, Michael Erb, Michael Eyb, Mathias Bartels, and Wolfgang Grodd, "Why Are Smiles Contagious? An fMRI Study of the Interaction between Perception of Facial Affect and Facial Movements," *Psychiatry Research* 123, no. 1 (2003), pp. 17–36. "Strategy #3, Find and Spread Positivity," discusses neurons that detect and return smiles. For more on this topic, see this article.

John Willis, "The Andon Cord," *IT Revolution*, December 18, 2020, https://itrevolution.com/kata/. "Strategy #4, Hear People Out," discusses assembly line cords at Toyota. The Toyota manufacturing "cord of accountability" is called an "Andon cord." You can learn much more about this cord and its history in Willis's article.

Lee Nelson, "How to Conduct a Head-to-Toe Assessment," Nurse.org, updated April 7, 2020, https://nurse.org/articles/how-to-conduct-head-to-toe-assessment/; Jean F. Giddens and Susan Wilson, *Health Assessment for Nursing Practice*, seventh edition (Netherlands: Elsevier, 2021). "Strategy #5, Step Back," discusses the head-to-toe assessment used by nursing and health-care professionals. For examples, see these articles.

Lewis R. Goldberg, "The Structure of Phenotypic Personality Traits," *American Psychologist* 48, no. 1 (1993) p. 26; Neil Fleming, "I'm Different; not Dumb. Modes of Presentation (VARK) in the Tertiary Classroom," in *Research and Development in Higher Education: Proceedings of the 1995 Annual Conference of the Higher Education and Research*

Development Society of Australasia (HERDSA), HERDSA, vol. 18, pp. 308–313. "Strategy #6, Communicate Clearly with One Another," mentions communication preferences based on personality traits and learning styles. Goldberg discusses personality traits, and Fleming discusses learning styles.

William Shakespeare, Romeo & Juliet, edited by Alan Durband (Hauppage, NY: Barron's, 1985); Bill Dubuque and Mark Williams, Ozark (Atlanta: Aggregate Films, 2017), Netflix, https://www.netflix.com/title/80117552. "Strategy #9, Set Aside Time for Problem Solving," references these works.

Alan Burdick, *Why Time Flies*, (NY: Simon & Schuster, 2017); Sylvie Droit-Volet, "Time Perception, Emotions, and Mood Disorders," *Journal of Physiology* 4 (2013), pp. 255–264. "Strategy #10, Make Better Use of Team Time," references scientific support for time-bending perceptions when feeling good or bad from these works.

Nancy Gahles, "The Physical Trauma of Grief and Loss," *Integrative Practitioner*, (November 22, 2016), https://www. integrativepractitioner.com/topics/news/body-trauma-grief; Antonio Lazzarino *et al.*, "The Association between Cortisol Response to Mental Stress and High-Sensitivity Cardiac Troponin T Plasma Concentration in Healthy Adults," *Journal of the American College of Cardiology* 62, no. 18 (2013), pp.

1694-1701; Bui, Eric, Emma Chad-Friedman, Sarah Wieman, Rachel H. Grasfield, Allison Rolfe, Melissa Dong, Elyse R. Park, and John W. Denninger. "Patient and provider perspectives on a mind–body program for grieving older adults." *American Journal of Hospice and Palliative Medicine*® 35, no. 6 (2018), pp. 858–865. "Strategy #14, Give Grief Its Space and Time," describes symptoms of grief in Dr. Gahles' article and the original source article by Lazzarino *et al.* The six guideposts are based on Dr. Bui and his team's work. They found that a specially designed, eight-week mind-body program can help reduce stress among older adults who have lost a spouse.

Internal Relationship Strategies

Alex Sandy Pentland, "The New Science of Building Great Teams," *Harvard Business Review* 90, no. 4 (2012), pp. 60–69. "Strategy #1, Encourage Team Member Bonding," discusses this article.

Tibor Bosse *et al.*, "Agent-based modelling of emotion contagion in groups," *Cognitive Computation Journal* 7 (2015), pp. 111–36; Brooks B. Gump and James A. Kulik, "Stress, Affiliation, and Emotional Contagion," *Journal of Personality & Social Psychology* 72, no. 2 (1997): 305–19. "Strategy #2, Have Fun and Laugh," discusses the idea that positive emotions are contagious and beneficial to people and teams.

Acorns, "About," April 14, 2021. https://www.acorns.com/about/. "Strategy #3, Value the Small Things," discusses the micro-investing firm Acorns.

Lutz Kaufmann and Claudia Wagner, *"Affective Diversity and Emotional Intelligence in Cross-functional Sourcing Teams," Journal of Purchasing and Supply Management* 23, no. 1 (2017), pp. 5–16. "Strategy #7, Respect One Another's Differences," mentions this article.

Aaron Ontiveroz, "Quarterback-less Broncos No Match for New Orleans: 'We Weren't Given a Chance,'" *The Denver Post* (November 29, 2020); Robert Sanders, "Researchers Find Out Why Some Stress Is Good for You," *Berkeley News* (April 16, 2013), https://news.berkeley.edu/2013/04/16/; Elizabeth D. Kirby *et al.*, "Acute Stress Enhances Adult Rat Hippocampal Neurogenesis and Activation of Newborn Neurons via Secreted Astrocytic FGF2," *eLife*, April 16, 2013, https://www.ncbi.nlm.nih.gov/pmc/articles/PMC3628086/. "Strategy #8, Focus on What the Group Can Control," discusses the game between the Broncos and the Saints on November 29, 2020, covered in Ontiveroz's article. For further information on the effects of stress, see Sanders's article and the original study by Elizabeth D. Kirby *et al.*

Mark Twain (Samuel L. Clemens) and Charles Dudley Warner, The Gilded Age: *A Tale of To-Day* (Hartford: American Publishing Company, 1874), 430. "Strategy #9, Tap in History, to a Degree," references Mark Twain's use of the phrase, "History never repeats itself," in this novel.

Mark Leary, "Why Do Hurt Feelings Hurt?", Lecture 9, Course No. 1626, *Understanding the Mysteries of Human Behavior*, The Teaching Company, 2012. "Strategy #12, Be Open to Feedback from Each Other," discusses the MRI evidence of the brain's efficient use of its pain centers for hurt feelings, as Duke University Professor Leary discusses in this lecture.

"Strategy #13, Have that Tough Conversation Directly," is based on a review of themes in the *Emotional Intelligence Appraisal – Team Edition* database. Teammates frequently comment on other teammates' circumventing direct conversations and the negativity this tactic creates as they complain, have side conversations, and fail to handle actual issues.

J. Keith Murnighan and Donald Conlon, "The Dynamics of Intense Work Groups: A Study of British String Quartets," *Administrative Science Quarterly* (1991), pp. 165–186; Karen Jehn and Elizabeth Mannix, "The Dynamic Nature of

Conflict: A Longitudinal Study of Intragroup Conflict and Group Performance," *Academy of Management Journal* 44 no. 2 (2001), pp. 238–251; Carsten De Dreu and Laurie Weingart, "Task versus Relationship Conflict, Team Performance, and Team Member Satisfaction: A Meta-Analysis," *Journal of Applied Psychology* 88, no. 4 (2003), p. 741; Jung, Malte F. "Coupling Interactions and Performance: Predicting Team Performance from Thin Slices of Conflict," *ACM Transactions on Computer-Human Interaction* (TOCHI) 23, no. 3 (2016), 1–32. "Strategy #14, Work Through a Conflict," discusses Murnighan and Conlon's work. *Relationship conflict* is defined by Jehn and Mannix. Relationship conflict is linked to lower team performance and member satisfaction by De Dreu and Weingart. The research on predicting low-performing teams within 15 minutes is discussed in "Coupling Interactions."

External Relationship Strategies

Rachel Rettner, "The Human Body: Anatomy, Facts & Functions" LiveScience.com, March 10, 2016, https://www.livescience.com/37009-human-body.html. "Strategy #1, Understand the Broader Environment," references how circulation flows according to this work.

LeaderEconomics.com Admin, "Teamwork Lessons from Pixar,

The British Red Cross and The Rolling Stones," LeaderEconomics.com, June 17, 2013, https://www.leaderonomics.com/articles/leadership/teamwork-lessons-from-pixar-the-british-red-cross-and-the-rolling-stones. "Strategy #2, Win Confidence with Quality Work," refers to this article.

Deborah Ancona and David Caldwell, "Demography and Design: Predictors of New Product Team Performance," *Organization Science* 3, no. 3 (1992), pp. 321–341. "Strategy #3, Leverage Team Member Relationship Strengths," discusses MIT types of communicators on diverse teams in this article.

Golden Gate Bridge, Highway and Transportation District, "History & Research," April 17, 2021 https://www.goldengate.org/bridge/history-research/; Jon Jecker and David Landy, "Liking a Person as a Function of Doing Him a Favour," *Human Relations* 22, no. 4 (1969): 371–78. "Strategy #5, Build Bridges," discusses the Golden Gate Bridge using information from this website and research on how doing someone a favor makes you like them by Jecker and Landy.

"The Timmy Awards," Tech in Motion, September 23, 2021 https://timmyawards.techinmotionevents.com. "Strategy #8, Celebrate Bigger," references this webpage.

Catherine Eley *et al.*, "The Leaning Tower of Pasta: Lessons in Team Performance and Creativity from a Core Surgical Training Boot Camp Design Challenge," *Journal of Surgical Education* 78, no. 5 (2021), pp. 1702–1708. "Strategy #10, Take Matters into Your Own Hands," discusses momentum in this article.

Andrew Moreau, "Little Rock Lab Offers Startups a Hand," *Arkansas Democrat Gazette* (July 18, 2021), https://www.arkansasonline.com/news/2021/jul/18/lr-lab-offers-startups-a-hand/. "Strategy #14, Tackle a Wider Problem," discusses the Rock It! Lab program showcased on the Central Arkansas Library System website. This program is discussed in Moreau's article.

Epilogue

Marjorie Shaw, "A Comparison of Individuals and Small Groups in the Rational Solution of Complex Problems," *The American Journal of Psychology* 44, no. 3 (1932), pp. 491–504. The earliest inklings of team emotional intelligence might even be traced back to 1932, when Shaw released a study showing that groups were better at problem-solving than individuals.

McCurdy and Lambert, "Efficiency."

Goleman, *Emotional Intelligence*; Travis Bradberry and Jean

Greaves', *The Emotional Intelligence Quick Book*, (New York: Simon & Schuster, 2005); Daniel Goleman, Richard E. Boyatzis, and Annie McKee, Primal Leadership: *Realizing the Power of Emotional Intelligence* (Boston: Harvard Business School, 2002). Goleman's book introduced the concept of emotional intelligence to the business world. A chapter on emotional intelligence in teamwork is discussed by Bradberry and Greaves. The emotional intelligence model by Goleman, Boyatzis, and McKee groups the four skills (self-awareness, self-management, social awareness, and relationship management) into the larger skills groups of personal and social competence. Our research confirms personal and social competence as the most accurate division of emotional intelligence into parts.

Bradberry and Greaves, *Emotional Appraisal – Team Edition*.

Alan Deutschman, "Change or Die," *Fast Company* 94 (May 2005); Carol S. Dweck, "Beliefs that Make Smart People Dumb," in *Why Smart People Can Be So Stupid*, edited by Robert Sternberg (New Haven: Yale University Press, 2003). Repeated practice leads to real change and results, as these two works discuss.

Monsoor Iqbal, "Zoom Revenue and Usage Statistics," Business of Apps, updated September 2, 2021, https://www.businessofapps.com/data/zoom-statistics/. Iqbal discusses Zoom user data.

Jeremy Bailenson, "Nonverbal Overload: A Theoretical Argument for the Causes of Zoom Fatigue," *Technology, Mind and Behavior* 2, no. 1 (2021). Bailenson discusses the five factors contributing to screen fatigue.

Daniel Goleman, Social Intelligence: *The Revolutionary New Science of Human Relationships* (New York: Bantam Dell, 2006). Social intelligence was introduced to the business world in this book.

Tim Shallice, Paul Burgess, and I. Robertson, "The Domain of Supervisory Processes and Temporal Organization of Behaviour [and Discussion]," *Philosophical Transactions: Biological Sciences* 351, No. 1346, (1996), pp. 1405–12. To learn more about how emotions function in the brain, see this article.

Bradberry and Greaves, *Emotional Intelligence 2.0*.

Vanessa Urch Druskat *et al.*, "Team Emotional Intelligence: Linking Team Social and Emotional Environment to Team Effectiveness," *Management and Organisation DIEM Scientific Journal* vol. 3, no. 1, (2017): 433–454; Vanessa Urch Druskat and Steven Wolff, "The Effect of Confronting Members Who Break Norms on Team Effectiveness, *Conflict in Organizational Teams*, edited by Leigh Thompson and Kristin

Behfar (Evanston: Northwestern University Press, 2006), pp. 229–260. For research on team norms as the basis for developing team emotional intelligence, start with this article by Urch Druskat et al. Earlier research on the difficulties of confronting teammates can be found in Urch Druskat and Wolff's article.

Sarah Sebo, Brett Stoll, Brian Scassellati, and Malte Jung, "Robots in Groups and Teams: A Literature Review," *Proceedings of the ACM Human-Computer Interaction* 4, no. CSCW2 (2020), pp. 1–36; Malte Jung, Nikolas Martelaro, and Pamela Hinds, "Using Robots to Moderate Team Conflict: The Case of Repairing Violations," *Proceedings of the Tenth Annual ACM/IEEE International Conference on Human-Robot Interaction* (March 2015), pp. 229–236; Filipa Correia et al., "Group-Based Emotions in Teams of Humans and Robots," *Proceedings of the ACM/IEEE International Conference on Human-Robot Interaction* (2018), pp. 261-269. These studies examine robot team members.

EQ RESOURCE GUIDE

The resource guide in the following pages provides more information about developing EQ within your team and across your organization.

TalentSmartEQ® also offers complimentary EQ resources including articles, white papers, webinars, and the Better EQ newsletter covering the latest EQ trends and developments in the workplace. You can subscribe for free at: **www.talentsmarteq.com.**

For additional training tools to improve your team EQ, please contact TalentSmartEQ at: **www.talentsmarteq.com/contact** or **1-888-818-7627**.

Team EQ Starts Now

You've learned how emotions within a team can get in the way of work—and how cultivating high team EQ can get your team on track. Now it's time to put these lessons into practice.

▼ **INTRODUCE** team EQ to your team to give everyone a common language for understanding and managing team emotions and relationships.

▼ **DEVELOP** an action plan with your team using the tools in this book and choose just one skill and three strategies to start with.

▼ **PRACTICE** intentionally and consistently.

Team EQ Action Plan

Select One Team EQ Skill and Three Team EQ Strategies:
Which of the four EQ skills will your group work on? Check one:

Team EQ Skill

_____Emotion Awareness

_____Emotion Management

_____Internal Relationships

_____External Relationships

Review the strategies for the team EQ skill your group selected. Then list up to three that your group wants to practice for a minimum of three months.

Team EQ Strategies to Practice

1._____

2._____

3. _____

Track Progress on Your Plan
Note the date your practice begins and note a date three months out to check in on your progress. Then, fill in the date your team agrees that it's time to move on to a new leg of your journey.

Dates to Track

_____Date started

_____Date to check in on progress

_____Date completed

Give Your Team an Extra Edge

Training programs that help hone EQ skills can give your team an extra edge. TalentSmartEQ's Mastering EQ® for Teams workshop elevates team EQ skills to help achieve peak performance by guiding team members to:

▼ **UNDERSTAND** what team EQ skills are and how to develop them.

▼ **MEASURE** their team EQ skills using the Emotional Intelligence Appraisal®—Team Edition to identify strengths and challenges.

▼ **DISCUSS** their team EQ results and strategies for navigating challenges that get in the team's way.

▼ **FORMULATE** a team EQ action plan and ground rules for working with each other moving forward.

There are two delivery options for the Mastering EQ for Teams Workshop:

We Train Your Team:
TalentSmartEQ® expert facilitators can conduct your session virtually for any intact team at your organization.

We Train the Trainer:
Attend an upcoming Mastering EQ® for Teams Train-the-Trainer session and begin facilitating this program internally at your organization.

....

Not sure if training would benefit your team? Visit **www.talentsmarteq.com/teamdiagnostic** and access TalentSmartEQ's complimentary diagnostic tool to see if your team is experiencing the types of challenges that can be addressed through training.

....

WORLD'S #1 PROVIDER OF EMOTIONAL INTELLIGENCE

Take Your Own EQ to the Next Level

EQ development isn't just for teams; it's also for individuals. Start your journey with the *Wall Street Journal* best-seller *Emotional Intelligence 2.0*. This book details TalentSmartEQ's revolutionary program to build your emotional intelligence and achieve your fullest potential.

This powerful guide, which includes complimentary access to TalentSmartEQ's Emotional Intelligence Appraisal®—Self Edition, will immediately help you:

- ▼ **LEARN** what behaviors are lifting you up or holding you back.

- ▼ **UNCOVER** the strategies most personally relevant to increasing your EQ.

- ▼ **TURN** insight into immediate action and lasting improvement.

In addition, TalentSmartEQ's suite of Mastering EQ® training solutions can show you how to harness the power of EQ at work and in life.

- Mastering EQ®—Level 1
- Mastering EQ®—Level 2
- Mastering EQ® for Teams
- Mastering EQ® for Hiring

Our clients find that continued practice, training, and coaching can increase EQ by an average of 7 points over 6-9 months.

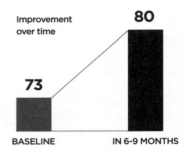

Improvement over time

80

73

BASELINE   IN 6-9 MONTHS

Why Focus on EQ in the Workplace?

EQ development is a foundational skill for addressing critical challenges your organization faces including: engaging employees, driving productivity, and navigating change. Stronger EQ skills in the workplace provide a competitive advantage by improving outcomes that are critical to your organization's culture:

▼ **Higher Productivity**

▼ **Increased Employee Engagement**

▼ **Improved Collaboration**

▼ **Ability to Navigate Change and Uncertainty**

▼ **More Effective Leadership**

▼ **Greater Resilience**

After EQ training, leaders at one of the largest U.S. not-for-profit health systems experienced a:

93% improvement in their **ability to handle conflict effectively**.

57% improvement in their **ability to deal effectively with change**.

54% improvement in their **ability to communicate clearly** and effectively.

Engineers at a Fortune 200 defense contractor experienced a:

40% improvement in their **ability to handle change effectively**.

26% improvement in the **quality of their relationships** with their coworkers.

For more insights about emotional intelligence, please visit **www.talentsmarteq.com**.

WORLD'S #1 PROVIDER OF EMOTIONAL INTELLIGENCE

Why TalentSmartEQ®

TalentSmartEQ® has spent over 20 years focused on bringing emotional intelligence research and skill development to the world.

**2 Million+
Assessments**

**75% Fortune
500 Served**

**2 Million+
Books Sold**

**35+ Countries
25+ Languages**

We have flexible tools to help individuals, teams, and entire organizations, and we use proven and practical approaches to meet your learners where they are.

▼ **We Can Train
Your Employees**

▼ **We Can Train
Your Trainers**

▼ **We Can Coach
Your Leaders**

What TalentSmartEQ® Customers Have Shared

Best training our company has ever had. I will never view a customer the same. This has helped with my relationships at home and my life.
— *Program Participant from a National Furniture Retailer*

Invaluable in identifying strengths and opportunities to improve your EQ. It helped me to apply direct strategies, improving my approach to work and my relationships each day.
— *Program Participant at a Global Financial Company*

One of the most valuable events in my professional training life...Thank you!
— *Certified Trainer from an Energy and Utilities Organization*

This program relates to real-life work experiences. It resonates with all types of personalities and employees, and it's totally universal across all levels and functions.
— *Executive at a Multi-national Retail Client*

The best, most impactful class our team has had the pleasure to teach!
— *Development Leader at a National Defense Organization*

For more information about TalentSmartEQ's emotional intelligence training solutions, please contact **www.talentsmarteq.com/contact** or call **888-818-6127**.